THE DUKE OF EDINBURGH AND I

THE DUKE OF EDINBURGH AND I

A shared love of carriage driving.

CHRISTINE SUSAN MAY

Copyright © 2024 by Christine May
All rights reserved.

No part of this book may be reproduced in any form or by any electronic or mechanical means, including information storage and retrieval systems, without written permission from the author, except for the use of brief quotations in a book review.

978-1-80541-542-8 – Paperback
978-1-80541-543-5 – Hardback
978-1-80541-541-1 – eBook

PREFACE

My body clock woke me at 6am on a beautiful sunny morning. It was dressage day. I had ponies to feed, manes to plait! I was competing in the carriage driving trials with my two ponies, Robin and Siggy, at Scone Palace, north of Edinburgh, Scotland. I went to feed my ponies their breakfast. The sun was low in the sky and slightly blinded me.

I saw the silhouette of a tall solitary man wandering in the yard.

It was HRH Prince Philip, the Duke of Edinburgh. He was enjoying the sunrise and the peace and quiet within the stable yard. The only sound was the horses snorting and chomping on their hay.

I said, "Good morning, sir". We briefly spoke about his book; I told him that I had a copy of it. Knowing that he had signed a few copies for other people, I boldly asked if he would sign my copy. As he is a tall man, and I was a mere 5ft 2 he seemed to look down at me.

Then, looking me up and down he replied, "I don't know you!"

I replied, "No sir, but I am a fellow carriage driver."

Then he said, "If you have it handy, but please hurry up, and do not tell anyone."

He graciously waited while I hurried to my room in the jockey's quarters to fetch it, which he kindly signed for me.

This book became my bible.

Competition Carriage Driving HRH The Duke of Edinburgh showing his signature, Philip more about this book later

ACKNOWLEDGEMENTS

His Royal Highness Prince Philip, Duke of Edinburgh for inspiring me to take up carriage driving and strive towards success: his love of horses shone through to me.

Sam Wilkinson, published writer, his encouragement was what I needed. His direction drew out my many memories. Some were painful, most were not. Sadly, Sam passed away before the book was published.

Mila For introducing me to Sam.

My sister Barbara for her encouragement.

My brother Stephen for helping me with accuracy.

*I dedicate this book to my family,
Lorna, Louise, and Fleur,
and my many dogs, cats, and horses
that have given me great pleasure.*

CONTENTS

Preface v
Acknowledgements vii

PART ONE

Early years 3
Luton 9
School years 13
When I was five 15
Now I am Six. 17
Pinchits and Whippets 19
The Tween years 23
My senior years, Denbigh Road school 25
London Gliding Club 31
The Pentecostal Church 35
My first Love 37
Teenage years continued 41
Growing up 43
Mods and Rockers 47
The Roger years 51
Moving to the Isle of Wight 55
My first pony 59

Stumbling at the first fence 63
Woodend Stud 67
Along came Richard. 71
The Hunt Master Popping Back in time
    For a Moment 75
Pride 79
Pride in my ponies 83
Back on the farm 87
Brighton driving trials 91
Stepping back in time 93
My Second Accident 97
The road to recovery 101
Fostering 103
National competitions 107
Developments and Dr. Snow 111
Fun at the end of the day 115
Eton collage and the film premier 117
The duke of Edinburgh and I 119
Windsor, Wembley, and the Pitney-Bowes 125
Hew Graham, seeking sponsorship. 129
The annual conference and
    Dr. Snow's research results 133
International competitions 135
Taking a break 141
Chinks in the Armour 145
Repairing the chinks 147
The demise of my marriage 151

CONTENTS

PART TWO

Me, who am I?.. 157
 Meeting Glen... 165
What to do next? The Movies!.. 171
I am now a famous Doctor. 179
My family, 1921–2021, A Full Century of
 Social History.. 181
My Mum.. 207
My extended family and Uncle Fred............................. 227
Lorna Jayne 231
Louise May... 245
Fleur May 263
My big brother Stephen.. 283
My sister, Barbara Avril 293
Me, my lodgers, and Glen 303
How Thailand and Kingsacre came about. 307
Dogs, my salvation 313
Moving on, a new life. 329
Returning to my roots. 329

About the author.. 337

Part One

CHAPTER ONE

Early years

There is a poem that I remember from a very young age. My mother used to recite it to me.

Written by A Milne,
the author of the Winnie the Pooh books
It is called *Now I am Six*.

When I was One, I had just begun.
When I was Two, I was nearly new.
When I was Three, I was hardly me.
When I was Four, I was not much more.
When I was Five, I was barely alive.
But now I am Six, I'm as clever as clever,
So, I think I'll be six now for ever and ever.

This poem was a model of my early years.

Born Christine Susan Ginn, in the front room of a modest terraced house in Lower Road, Eastbourne on June 25, 1948, the youngest of three. Life was good in my early years. We played freely in the street, without a care in the world.

Across the road was my grandfather's blacksmith shop with its great shire horses coming and going. These huge creatures captivated my imagination with their size, power, and an undeniably gentle side to their nature.

Looking back, in my early years, life was good playing in that street. We had no toys; we didn't need them. We had our friends and we had each other while playing all sorts of street games. The streets in those days were gaslit and a man came with a long stick with a flame on it to fire them up each evening. In the morning, he would come back and snuff them out.

There were no cars then. Lower Road was a *cul de sac*, so we were perfectly safe. Mum used to half joke that it was a dead-end street and therefore it was no surprise that we found ourselves there, a bunch of dead-end kids going nowhere. We were working class and should not expect to make anything of ourselves. Our 'birthright' was to live in a dead-end situation. No!

Remembering the heat of the summer, we played with tar bubbles on the newly laid street, bursting them and getting splattered, black, and sticky. Mum, ever patient, would get the mess off of us. She rubbed our hands with butter until the tar softened and was removed. Then she would wash our hands with soap and water without any admonishment in the slightest form.

We never knew what was beyond the alleyway or what was over the mysterious high flint wall at the end of the street. It was unknown territory for us little ones. Being the youngest, it was my fate to just follow others around, often getting in the way. You could say that was a deliberate ploy to make myself a nuisance and, in the end, it worked, and I was begrudgingly 'let in'.

We often played hopscotch, writing on the road with a lump of chalk from the garden, fashioning a numbered grid. We would throw a stone onto the grid starting at number one, then hop onto the square, slowly getting to number six, then we would turn and hop all the way back again. Another favourite was marbles. We would collect coloured glass marbles, then with our friends we would nudge our marble into a small hole in the road in the fewest moves to find a winner, sometimes trading a favourite one with a friend.

The girls would play skipping, singing songs as we jumped. Then there was always hide and seek where one person had to close their eyes and count to ten, announcing loudly, "coming, ready or not!" I especially loved to play *Ally Ally Oh*. We would hold hands in a chain, one girl would put her hand on a wall to form an arch way, and then we would skip round and under the arch singing *'The big ship sailed through the ally ally oh'* until we all had our arms folded across our chests, job well done! Innocent trouble-free days

My grandfather, in his blacksmith shop, forged all the ornate steel railings around the old town as well as the huge gates to the lovely Motcombe Gardens. But come the 1940s they were removed and used in the war effort. After the war he rebuilt them all, they still stand to this day, a testimony to his life and work.

Barbara and Stephen and I, standing against the railings that Granddad made in Motcombe park, with Neptune.

CHRISTINE SUSAN MAY

*Mum with Fleur and Aunty Dorothy
By the pond in Motcombe park*

CHAPTER TWO

LUTON

When I was Three

In 1952 just before my 4th birthday, the family moved from Eastbourne, the seaside town of my birth, to Leagrave, Luton, Bedfordshire. Mum and us three children moved first, Dad followed on later.

Our new home was one of only four semi-detached houses in the street, Wickstead Avenue ran through open fields that were made of small pebble-dashed houses. Later, new houses were built along the road to accommodate the police force, so from then on, we were expected to behave ourselves.

But still, back then the house was surrounded by open fields of grassland and brambles that provided us with blackberries which Mum turned into jam. We used to go out with Dad into the countryside to find 'crab apple' trees, too; these apples were perfect to add to the blackberry jam.

A favourite activity of ours was to stand on the Roman road bridge where we watched the trains pass underneath, and we would dance madly in the steam that came gushing up around us. Once a day the 'Flying Scotsman' train to Scotland whizzed under the bridge

One day my brother Stephen and I were playing tag in the street, when the boy from next door joined us. He was 'it', so he had to chase after us, trying to catch one of us to tag. As he was walking backwards, he turned round and split his head open on a lamp post. Stephen saw the blood and fainted. An ambulance was called and took Stephen away instead of the lad with the cut on his forehead!

As a child I was driven by an overwhelming instinct that I could not yet quite put my finger on. All I knew was that I had a very strong desire to find and rescue animals in distress. From an early age wandering away from home was the norm for me, looking for lost or stray animals. It wasn't unknown for me to bring a cat home, I hid the cat in the coal shed.

When the surrounding fields were developed for housing, I remember that we climbed inside the new structures on the building site to play. We used to lay planks along the ground, pretending they were bridges, and each side was jungle, infested with crocodiles. Once I fell and cut my shin; I told Mum that a crocodile bit me.

The whole setup was a dirty place with rubble and the usual detritus of a building project, but the smells of newly plastered walls and wet paint were familiar and somehow comforting. If we found a ladder, we would put it up against the wall, so that we could explore the upstairs—staircases were the last things to be installed.

But eventually front doors were added, which meant that we could no longer get in and explore.

CHAPTER THREE

School years

When I Was Four

I was enrolled in the Beechwood Road School Nursery at four years of age. It was called the Green Nursery. My route to school meant traversing fields, and squeezing through railings to get in.

It was scary to be with children who were not my family. This is where we were taught how to interact with other children and to be socially aware. We were taught the Lord's prayer, the ABC and to count up to the number ten. We learned how to share toys and take turns, and we were also expected to have an afternoon nap on mattresses on the floor in the main hall. It was all very formal to me.

And then there were the starchy and formal school dinners during which we were taught how to eat properly, using a knife and fork.

I didn't like it very much.

CHAPTER FOUR

When I was five

I was Barely Alive

At the age of five years, the move over to the Blue Nursery was wonderful because there was a rocking horse! Share! Share! What did they mean? I didn't understand that word! I simply did not want to share it with anyone. I Insisted on wearing my new cowgirl outfit to school and went in early so that I could ride on it before anyone else. So 'bags it'. Yes, no points guessing that this behaviour was a portent of the future.

Again, we were expected to take a nap in the afternoons. School dinners were awful. Once we were served salad. I refused to eat the lettuce as it made me feel sick, so the teacher made me sit at a table on my own and told me that I would stay there till I had eaten it. I sat there all afternoons! I never did eat it.

In later years, Mum told me that once, after putting my brother and sister to bed, she had to go out looking for me, a neighbour told Mum that she had seen me down in the park, three miles away. I was only five years old.

There was a street party in Wickstead Avenue for all the children.

I still don't know what it was all about (perhaps it was the coronation of the queen). It didn't matter in the slightest to me, but it would figure largely in my later life. We had delicious cucumber sandwiches along with jelly and cake, and that's what counted.

I am sitting bottom left

CHAPTER FIVE

Now I am Six.

At the age of six, my transfer into the main school building made me feel grown up. Finding my feet at last. That was when I re-joined Stephen and Barbara who were in higher classes than me. That made me feel like I was back in the fold.

I don't remember having any special friends in those days and rarely was school enjoyable. I had the feeling that there were far more exciting things in life that could be done. Whenever the opportunity arose, or if I was paying a visit to the toilet, my coat was calling to me; hanging on a peg near the open door; it was just too tempting—I would just go home. When skiving off school, it was very simple to tell my Mum I was such a good girl that they had let me go home early. Mum never questioned this rather twisted logic.

Once, the day after I had absconded, I asked mum to walk me to school. Mum overheard a lady saying, "Is that the little girl who ran away from school yesterday? No-one sent out a search party to look for me.

CHAPTER SIX

Pinchits and Whippets

Once, in the park I saw a lady accompanied by a brown dog. It seemed to me that it was running faster than the wind; it was a captivating sight. As I was showing great interest in this dog, the lady started chatting to me. She told me what sort of dog it was.

I was so excited I rushed home to tell my mother about this dog. On telling Mum it was called a 'pinchit,' Mum stopped whatever she was doing at the time and laconically asked, "Do you mean a whippet?" That started my love affair with whippets.

Around about this time I acquired a push bike, which I painted blue. The bike enabled me to go out cycling for miles just looking for horses. Armed with a slice of bread and some string for a halter I climb on their backs and would just sit there for hours. No one ever knew where to find me. My mother found out about my horse-seeking wanderings, but instead of telling me off, she said that she would buy me a safety helmet!

At the age of twelve I saw an ad in the local newspaper shop for a dog walker. It didn't take long for me to get there. I was just like a whippet, greased lightning. In no time at all I was there on the doorstep. Lo and behold this man, Mr. Salter, had no less than five whippets! I was in heaven! So that was my after-school job—walking these dogs, Skipper, Solo, Badger, Candy, and Dolly. I groomed them and even cleaned their teeth, and shook their blankets, not minding how long it all took. To get paid two shillings and sixpence for the privilege was unbelievable!

Not long after, there was a notice in the corner shop advertising horse-riding lessons. My world was almost complete. The following Saturday, there I was joining a queue of hopefuls to get a fifteen-minute ride for two shillings and sixpence, my weekly earnings from walking Mr. Salter's whippets.

However, on getting to the front of the queue, I was told that the arrangement was a week in hand. As I did not have five shillings, I would have to come back the next week. All the same they took my money! Quite frankly, they wanted to stop for the day, because the 3 ponies were worn out. Needless to say, the following Saturday guess who was first in the queue—me!

I quickly realized that, to be the first person there enabled me to stay all day leading the ponies around, something I loved very much, so you could say that I paid, yet got paid in kind.

CHAPTER SEVEN

The Tween years

With my two best friends, Jean and Mary, I joined the Girl Guides. Their meetings were held in Beechwood School.

Once we got into the science room and made a small fire! It was just another adventure for us. We never intended any harm; we just wanted to be dare devils. The next day there was a delicious rumour going around that 'someone' had broken into the science lab and had tried to burn it down. We tried to hold back our laughter all day.

In the school holidays, my sister, my two friends and I, went into the school grounds through the railings, and climbed up the trellis to get up on to the roof. We sat astride the apex pretending to be on horseback, then slid down the other side to run around the quadrangle corridor until the caretaker came out and shouted at us. This was my eleventh year.

Later that day when I went home, entering via the back door, my mother casually told me that our next-door neighbour had seen me on the school roof! A shrug of the shoulders said it all. Now, if all this seems to be shockingly bad behaviour for an eleven-year-old English schoolgirl in the 1950s, I never once saw a look of horror or anger on my mother's face, leading me to believe that it was quite all right to do anything I wanted. As previously said, I had no concept of right or wrong.

At a parents' evening my teacher told my mother that I had expressed a wish to be a kennel maid. She said, "If I were you, I'd let her do it because she doesn't seem to have an academic brain- cell in her head!"

Life carried on as 'normal' for me, riding, walking the whippets, going down the marsh to meet up with my friends. That summer, life was good.

CHAPTER EIGHT

My senior years, Denbigh Road school

Predictably enough, failing my eleven-plus exams saw me off to the secondary modern school, Denbigh Road, a bus ride away. The fare was one penny each way. I was given sixpence to last the week, I had the choice to walk home some days and use the bus other days but I chose to walk all the time, and saved the money for other things. Now I was twelve, and was still walking Mr. Salters' whippets, my pocket money slowly increased.

My brother, the clever one, was already at Denbigh Road school and was Head Boy. My sister was in the commercial class learning shorthand and typing as it was considered that 'ladies' should become secretaries or office staff.

Despite my wantonness and stubborn behaviour someone there must have had 'high hopes' for me because 'the powers that be' put me into a class above my ability. This did not sit well with me. I was away from my friends, it made me unhappy, and I was out of my depth. Thankfully, after half term the hierarchy sent me down.

However, my friends had re-grouped. Something had to be done to get back into my circle. Therefore, being very rebellious towards my 'Head Boy' brother, I refused to walk in single file or stop chattering. That did the trick! My friends came back under my umbrella.

One day the owner of the riding club where my Saturdays were spent, told me that she was going to sell one of the horses. Instantly a book was set up to raise money to buy it. A huge two shillings and sixpence was raised! In spite of everything, that did not deter me; I still hoped that, one day the garden shed would house a horse; imaginary or real it would be fed from the grass on the verges of the road.

I put it about that I owned a horse. A cheeky 'know it all' girl called me a liar. What? A red mist came over me! I invited her to come and see 'it,' my newly acquired steed. The shed was empty of course so I stormed down the garden to where my Mum was hanging out the washing, placed my hands firmly on my hips, and accused her of letting my horse escape!

We were, with the notable exception of my father, an animal-loving family. We went to the RSPCA to adopt a little dog called Judy. When we saw her at the shelter, she was sweet and friendly, but once home, she morphed into a little tyrant. She would sit on the sofa and snap and snarl at anyone who tried to get her off. On coming home from school, it was my duty to take Judy out.

Mum was never in; she was always working hard in the grocery store. I would make myself a jam or Marmite sandwich and take Judy down to the marsh, a riverside open area with swings and roundabouts. Sitting on a swing, I'd invite a boy to give me a push (Judy was always on my lap). When the boy came to push me, she would leap at him, much to my delight.

It was always after dark when I wandered home, but no-one worried if Judy was with me; I was quite safe. Mum never asked me where we had been. Dad was always hard at work in the shed, so I never saw him. He was *forever* working in that shed.

After a very full day, **it was early to bed for me, so that I could dream.**

After a year at the senior school, the only lessons that were any good for me were geography and art. During that time, my friend Jean and I would always sit together and share pencils, rubbers, and rulers. One day the teacher, Mrs. Wood, made Jean move to another seat three rows behind. We weren't allowed to talk to each other, so it became necessary to write messages on my desk lid, such as 'pass the ruler' and 'Woody is a sod.' At the end of the lesson, we all went out to play.

Very soon a prefect collared me and escorted me back into the classroom. Mrs. Wood said, "Did you write that?" pointing at the message on my desk. She angrily pointed out to me that it was written in biro (you were only allowed to use fountain pens, not biros). I was the only person in the class who used a biro, so it was a double whammy for me. My reply was an emphatic, "No". However, it was a bit of a waste of time denying it! But deny it, I did. She sent me to ask the headmaster to come to the classroom. He asked the same question, and my answer was the same. He told me to go and stand outside his office. Standing there all day was very boring. Mr. Whitaker had two lights above his office door, a red and a green one. Every time the green light came on, it was a signal for me to go into his office and he would pose the same question repeatedly. My answer was always the same.

I stood there for a total of three days. To make a change, Mr. Whitaker sent me to fetch one of the boy prefects. We stood in front of his desk, and he pointed at his wastepaper bin and said, "Look! It's on fire!" The boy ran out! Stunned, I stared at the bin thinking that he had lost his mind somewhere along the trail until, the penny dropped; it was a fire drill! The prefect had already activated the fire alarms and he was now running up around the boys' corridors shouting *Fire! Fire!* before running up to the girls' end of school to do the same (at that time the boys and girls were segregated at our school, with the boys up one end and the girls up the other).

The next day it was back to standing outside his door. By Friday, fed up with this fiasco, I finally admitting that the stupid message was mine. Mr. Whittaker promptly frog-marched me to the art room, where my class was having a lesson. He pompously announced to the class that he was going to cane me for telling lies. And he did! 'Six of the best,' three whacks on each hand. My sentence was also announced during Monday morning assembly. After school it was off to the woodwork room to plane the desk lid down until the writing was gone.

CHAPTER NINE

London Gliding Club

In his leisure time Dad was a glider pilot. He was building a new style two-seater glider in our huge shed. He named it 'the Kestrel' and this was going to be a training glider to help aspiring pilots. He did this from scratch. This glider now sits in a hanger in a museum in Wattisham, Lincolnshire.

We were spending nearly all our weekends up at the London Gliding Club at Dunstable where Dad had a workshop. He used to recover crashed gliders and rebuild them back to certificate-of- air-worthiness standard.

With regards to the glider that Dad was building, Stephen was expected to work with him after school. Stephen was most certainly not allowed out with his two best friends, Stephen Baker, and Ron Burgess. When they came to call for him. my father would just send them away.

Often, my friends, Mary and Jean, came with me to the gliding club at the weekends. As soon as we got bored, we would trek the 10 miles home. But it was not all total boredom. In a field close to the gliding club, there was a horse in the field. This horse was huge, far too big for me to get on; so, I was content to just brush it. We named it Beauty and we considered it to belong to us.

Twelve years old at the time, I was a wild child doing crazy things in dangerous situations. I never considered myself in any danger, although we did once see a man jiggling with himself behind a bush in front of us, but we just laughed it off and ran away!

In 1961, when I was thirteen, my father left us. He had already been gone for a week before I realized he'd left; I hadn't even noticed. At that tender age, the connotations of what had happened went straight over my head. Apparently, he had gone off with a woman who had three children. Still, because I rarely saw anything of him it hardly changed my life. Some years later, when I was having one of my many emotional peaks and lows, I was chucking stuff into an overnight bag and I drove off from home in Chichester, to Luton, to my sister's house. Having a long chat, Barbara detected my anxiety and told me that she wasn't surprised by my desire to 'cut and run' every time the going got tough. Her explanation was revealing to say the least.

"It's not the least surprising after what Dad used to do to you."

"What are you talking about?" was my response.

"He used to spank you every week on a regular basis; it was, 'tonight is spanking Christine night'."

I had no recollection of this whatsoever. It shocked me!

After dad left, Mum worked at the Electrolux factory. It was now that terrible winter of 1963, when the snow came and then stayed for what seemed like forever. We had no electricity and life was difficult, we had a coke-burning stove in the back room, and I distinctly remember huddling around that stove to get dressed. We used to put our clothes inside the bedclothes as we slept to keep warm and placed our coats on top as an extra insulation blanket.

One day, at the age of 14, I had a brilliant idea; I decided to treat Mum and the family to a roast chicken and veg dinner for when Mum came home from work for her midday lunchbreak. She was shocked. At the time the police were cruising the streets with loudspeakers warning everyone not to use house gas because of the danger. That dinner was delicious…

CHAPTER TEN

THE PENTECOSTAL CHURCH

When I was 12 years old, while walking along a road, I saw a group of teenagers clustered in and around a hut. This turned out to be a Pentecostal church youth club, and it looked interesting and inviting. 'Nosy me' went in and was welcomed. I sat with the others on benches as they proclaimed slogans like 'God is Love' ; it was easy to just copy them—a small price to pay for some communal fun.

Every Thursday for months I went along, and it was all quite good fun. Then it was announced that there was going to be a summer camp in Derbyshire, near the Blue John mines. I was up for it but it required Mum's consent. Mum said that I could go. It was impressive: we slept in big brown teepee-type tents and went for daily outings. Sunday dawned and we were all called into the main marquee for morning prayers. There was a huge circle of chairs, and we all sat down and were told that a very special minister was coming to baptize us. What was that all about?

Sure enough, this man arrived and went around the circle of chairs laying his hands on children's heads. This terrified me, it was so strange. When he arrived at the back of my seat, he placed his hands on my head, and all I could think of was that I just wanted him to get them off me! I instinctively copied the other kids who made strange noises. He shook my head and shouted, "let it out, my child". I simply cannot describe how disturbing it was! I arrived back home, not wanting to talk about it, and not wanting to ever go back to youth club again.

A lady representative came to collect me one day for a meeting and told Mum that she should make me give up horse riding on Sundays and go to church instead. I refused to come out of my bedroom, or explain why! Game over! **I have been wary of religion** ever since.

CHAPTER ELEVEN

My first Love

At fourteen I noticed a good-looking lad around our street, and there I was, falling hopelessly in love with Stephen Dillingham. It was inevitable. He was sixteen. He looked fantastic in drainpipe jeans, a leather jacket, winklepicker shoes and an Elvis Presley quiff.

It was true love; we went out most evenings, just wandering around arm in arm, stopping to kiss and cuddle. If it was raining, we would go down an alleyway to kiss and stay dry. I couldn't imagine life without him, I got engaged to be married to him on my 15th birthday. Crazy but true! In hindsight I don't think I have ever truly loved anyone else.

Stephen and I learned a jive routine in his mother's front room and went to dances in the hall of Beachwood Road School. In those days we girls used to wear very full skirts with lots of stiff petticoats underneath so that they swung out when we spun around. Those were heady, halcyon days; days of adventure and fascination for both of us.

I taught Stephen how to ride horses. We shared most things; a love of riding horses was just one. We used to hire two ponies for the day and ride over to my mum's house. Stephen and I even rode the ponies to meet her once as she came out of the Electrolux factory for the lunchtime break. My pony reared up at the sight of hundreds of people pouring out of the factory gates towards us.

It was a torrid affair. Eventually Stephen left school to work in an ironmonger's shop in Luton. One day I was going there to see him at work, but I stopped dead in my tracks when I saw him. He was wearing a brown two-thirds length overall jacket Just like that, my bubble burst. My winkle picking rock boyfriend disappeared in a puff of smoke! I suddenly imagined myself living in a flat or a council house married to a shop assistant! Not that I'm a snob. At sixteen it all went wrong for me and ending it all was inevitable. It was a painful thing for me to do. More painful, it would seem to be, for Stephen.

I came home from school one day in despair, overwhelmed by grief for what might have been. My world had crashed and burned. I was sobbing so loud that Mrs. Gray from next door came around to see what was wrong. She comforted me saying 'boyfriend troubles'. No more was said.

Stephen and I outside Mum's house In Wickstead Avenue

CHAPTER TWELVE

Teenage years continued

As I mentioned before, my brother Stephen was the intelligent member of the family, and as such we were not allowed comics. Stephen had to read the broadsheets instead. We had no TV and no toys. I didn't need toys and had never heard of television! This made me resentful towards Stephen at times, but being too young to recognize this emotion, it didn't stop me from swiping and hitting out at him if the mood took me. How it made me feel! Stephen was a quiet and gentle teenager. During my onslaughts, he would simply cover up his face. Looking back now, I feel ashamed; I can see the bigger picture.

I left school, aged 15 years to work in a ladies' clothes shop in town. Learning the art of window dressing, I felt grown up at last. I earned one pound ten shillings per week; the one pound was given to Mum for my keep.

One day a message came from my father to say that he wanted to buy me a horse! Well, all my Christmases seemed to have come together at once that day. There

I was, looking in the weekly paper, to find the first available horse for sale. Then it was meeting my father to see it, desperately wanting it, only to be told that if Dad bought it for me, it would be on the condition that I give his stepchildren riding lessons. The short answer to that was either it was mine and mine alone, or it was simple—he could keep his money, I didn't want it.

CHAPTER THIRTEEN

Growing up

My new stepfather, Ted, moved in via the back door, so to speak. From then on I became unruly and defiant. This was one of the reasons that it became necessary for me to leave home at sixteen.

Leaving home to live in a bedsit in town, I felt liberated. I also left the job in the ladies' outfitters, to work in the Ballito stocking factory, which put more money in my pocket, but oh! it was a soul-destroying job; I hated the work and was frightened of the older workers who bullied me to the point where even going to the restroom scared me in case they followed me. Thankfully, I got a better paid part-time job as the first ever female petrol pump attendant in the area, and those difficulties were left behind me.

Having left home and gained a degree of independence I met a bloke who lived near my bedsit—a new relationship was on the cards. Knowing of my love for animals, he stupidly bought me a snake in a glass tank. The wretched thing used to strike at the glass each time

I put the kettle on. Enough was enough! I took it back to the pet shop to get the money back; however, the pet shop offered to exchange it for a little brown puppy—no contest. The pet shop owner told me to go back the following week to collect its pedigree certificate. Guess what? She was a whippet. I named her Sherry. I took her with me everywhere, including to work on the bus. She spent all the afternoons sleeping in a box in my kiosk. We were inseparable.

After living in the bedsit for about 10 months, it became obvious that my health was beginning to suffer, mainly because I was burning the candle at both ends, so my family GP, Dr Seed, suggested that I moved back home with Sherry. There was a certain routine back in my life. Also, it was a good idea to leave behind the man whom I had been seeing.

I decided to take Sherry to dog shows. I had to teach her how to stand in a show pose and began by getting her to stand on the table. Ted told me to get 'it' off the table or he would knock 'it' off. Sweeping Sherry into my arms, I looked up and Ted was holding his fist above me. I dared him to go ahead and hit me, saying I would take myself straight off to the police station if he did. He was so angry with me and proclaimed that he would willingly go to prison for me. Ted and I just didn't get on; we were always at loggerheads with each other.

At seventeen I started to take driving lessons. Rather conveniently for me, the instructor became my new boyfriend! At the time he owned a turquoise Hillman Imp, which was also the car that was used for my lessons. It gave me the opportunity to drive a lot as I insisted on driving everywhere we went, whenever the opportunity arose. I passed my test and obtained my driving license for the first time with flying colours, the first member of our household to do so.

CHAPTER FOURTEEN

MODS AND ROCKERS

The sixties were an iconic era. Colours and music exploded, black cars morphed into blue or green, ballads turned into anthems of love and peace, skirts shortened to mini-length and bright-coloured clothes were the in-thing. This blossomed into a new age for fashion. Hot pants followed miniskirts, and flared bell bottom jeans superseded the drain-pipe jeans.

The winter of 1963 was the coldest for 200 years. It began abruptly just before Christmas in 1962. The weeks before had been changeable and stormy, but then on 22nd December a high-pressure system moved to the north-east of the British Isles, dragging bitterly cold winds across the country.

My best friend, Mary, married a black US Marine. They met at a Saturday night dance held at the US Air Force base, near where we lived. As a bride she wore white hotpants, and after the wedding she went with Lionel to live in the United States of America. She was subjected to reverse race hate and abuse. At that time such mixed marriages were considered very 'risqué,' but then Mary was always considered to be a trendsetter. Mary and I stayed connected over the years by letter. Sadly, she developed brain cancer, and eventually she died of it. She donated her body to science.

And of course, this was the beginning of the Mods and Rockers era. The Rockers wore drainpipe jeans and winklepicker shoes. The boys would invariably sport leather jackets and an Elvis hair- cut, with slicked-back sides and a greasy quiff. They were tough boys. Their girlfriends either dressed sort of the same, or wore blouses, flared skirts that stood out with colourful starched net petticoats underneath and had bouffant hairstyles. We would pose on street corners, sitting side saddle on the motorbikes, smoking, or like me, just pretending to smoke.

The Mods were just the opposite! They were called woolly woofters by us Rockers. They rode motor-scooters, and wore straight trousers, brothel creeper loafer-type shoes, colourful jumpers and long parka coats with a fur-lined hood. Their hair was neat and short, often styled after the Beatles' early hairstyle. They would have an aerial at the back of their Italian-themed scooters, usually with a fox tail flying from it like a symbol.

Word would get out where they were meeting. Of course, no one had a mobile phone back then but believe me, word got around all the same. The Rockers would get together and disrupt the Mods' meetings simply by strutting about in their leather jackets, looking tough. There was a huge meeting held on Brighton seafront by the Mods, some of whom rode for hundreds of miles to be there. The Rockers got wind of it and went down to Brighton. This time there was serious fighting in the streets which lasted for two days, moving along the coast to Hastings and back.

Steve Dillingham and I were definitely Rockers!

CHAPTER FIFTEEN

THE ROGER YEARS

After the heartbreak with Stephen Dillingham, I concluded that true love did not exist. It was a fantasy, an illusion that didn't last forever. Indeed, it was necessary to have respect which would take over once the initial passion subsided. This played out later in life with all my relationships.

Working as a petrol pump attendant gave me lots of opportunities to meet men. It was about this time that Roger drove into the petrol station. He had a swanky brand-new Morris Oxford estate and was ten years older than me. He asked me out, so he became my Tuesday, Thursday and Saturday date, with Saturdays being dance night. We went to the dance hall, where Roger tried his hand at some ballroom with me; it came across as 'old fashioned and stuffy' (if only 'Strictly Come Dancing' was about then!).

Slowly I began dropping all my other suitors. I only went out with Roger; he seemed to fulfil my criteria for a steady and dependable man. I can still remember being sixteen, going on seventeen, and feeling the thrill I got when Roger drove us up the newly built M1 motorway at 100 miles an hour, and afterwards, stopping at the Toddington Road motorway services for coffee. Almost no one of our age drank alcohol in those days; we always met up at coffee shops with a juke box and drank 'frothy coffee'.

Sometimes we went dancing at the Mecca ballroom. It was all rather romantic while it lasted, with waltzes and quicksteps being the order of the day. The disco was a long way off yet. On the way home we would pull into a country layby for a kiss and cuddle on the back seat. Sure, enough I got pregnant. I had no concept of how that had happened. This was 1966, the days of unmarried mothers' homes. Adoption by strangers was a scary thought. I was terrified of having to tell my mum but eventually I did. Characteristically she just said, "Who is it?" and "Are you getting married?" The answer was yes, so she then said, "We can't make it this week because it's too soon, nor next week because it's Easter." So, in three weeks it was down to the registry office, married and living with my in-laws.

My Mum had agreed for me to have my baby at her house, because I was terrified of hospitals. Lorna Jayne was born on October 21st at 10pm, delivered by our family doctor, Dr Seed, in my mother's bedroom. At the time I felt like the Mother Mary with this beautiful child, until the next day when the news was full of the Aberfan disaster where so many children had died. Believing that 'for every life there is a death' the 'Baby Blues' set in. This was the beginning of a lifetime of depression that was not diagnosed in those days.

When Lorna was three weeks old, we, Roger, me, and our baby moved back into my in-laws' house, under strict orders to keep the baby quiet. I spent many hours walking the streets with Lorna in a pram, trying to keep her crying from disturbing the family. By the time she was six-months old, I knew we desperately needed a house of our own. We used my savings of £250 as a deposit, and Roger sold his precious car and bought a Morris Minor van for work.

He had worked for the Eastern Electricity Board for fifteen years, and this had fuelled the thought in me of him being steady and dependable; this was one reason that I respected him. Because my spinning relationship with Stephen Dillingham ended so tragically I had come to the state of mind at an early age that love did not really exist. Respect was the key to a lasting marriage; a strange and cynical concept for someone so young.

I enjoyed being a wife and mother, keeping the house clean and tidy. Mondays was washing day. Not having a washing machine, I had to wash the sheets and clothes by hand in the sink. Then there was cake baking day when I dedicated the whole day to making enough Victoria sponge cakes and fruit loaf to last the week, which were kept in a chest freezer. Afternoons were spent walking Sherry the whippet, with Lorna in a push chair.

CHAPTER SIXTEEN

Moving to the Isle of Wight

When Lorna was two, my sister, Barbara, married Richard, who had spent many summer holidays over on the Isle of Wight. He loved it over there. Barbara and Richard subsequently moved over to live on the Isle of Wight. Barbara suggested that we moved over there, too.

We talked it over and concluded that it would be good for Lorna to grow up there in the countryside near the sea, away from urban life. We bought a bungalow off plan for £4,200. Roger got a job as an electrician and moved over there, leaving me to sell the Sunden Park home. It took three months to sell. During that time, I was alone. I worked evenings stacking shelves at Sainsburys to earn money to buy the essential things in life, while Grandmother Ginn babysat for me. During those three months it dawned on me that the move was going to be a very scary prospect. It did not sit well with me. I didn't want to go to the Isle of Wight. As far as I was concerned, it might as well have been Australia. It was, after all, over the water! It was a place where I'd never been; it was outside of my comfort zone.

During this time, I tried to meet up with Stephen Dillingham for a coffee and chat. I guess I was wishing for forgiveness somehow. He declined to see me.

The day dawned when Roger came back to Luton, bringing the removal men with him. I informed Roger that I'd changed my mind, I didn't want to go. It was too late! He replied, "If you don't come with me, you will never see a penny of the money."

I hot footed it around to my mother's house to ask for help, telling her that I didn't want to go. Mum's answer was, "You can't stay here. You've made your bed, so now go and lie in it." So that's what I did. I settled into my self-constructed bed; I had no choice but to lay in it, eventually admitting that some parts of the mattress were sort of okay.

Yes, it was in the countryside and near the sea. I had a blank canvas of a garden to work on and landscape, and I kept busy being creative, keeping our new home clean and tidy with the usual washing and baking day still part of my routine. It was just like the old song!

> My old man said follow the van and don't dilly-dally on the way.
> Off went the van with my home in it,

I followed on with my old cock linnet
I dillied, I dallied, I dallied and I dillied.
Lost my way and don't know where to roam.

CHAPTER SEVENTEEN

My first pony

I never forgave Roger for his threat to keep my money. After moving across the sea to the Isle of Wight, I worked part-time as a waitress and bar maid and this allowed me to save all my money for my own horse, which I intended to have one day. I was 20 years old, and still had that elusive dream. When at last there was £70 in the kitty, I took Lorna with me for the day, and we went from Freshwater to Lymington on the ferry, hoping beyond hope to find a New Forest pony to buy. At this time Lorna was just two years old. We traipsed around seeing nothing, so I asked a local where could anyone buy a pony? He gave me the telephone number of a man who could help, and we went back home to re-organize ourselves.

Later, I phoned the man in question and tried to explain that my choice was a liver chestnut pony. He claimed to have at least 130 ponies, so we arranged to meet. I went over on my own this time. He met me at the ferry in his Land Rover and we drove around to see various locations. I told him I was disappointed to not see any chestnut ponies, and only then did he admit that he didn't have one. What! Then I saw the most magnificent pony ever, I had spotted one! He explained that it was a six-year-old stallion, called Chief.

Chief had been annually graded. Grading the stallions that ran free in the new Forest was a way of keeping the breed pure, and therefore he was easy to handle. It was a done deal. This was the one for me. **We** drove back to his farm, where he sent his two sons out on horse-back to catch Chief. The man offered to keep him for a week in order to have him gelded and broken. No way! I wanted him there and then.

So 'Fernhill Chief ' was loaded into a canvas top pig transporter and taken down to the Lymington car ferry. The captain agreed to me walking him onto the car deck, on the strict understanding, that the pony was quiet and broken. Despite him being rounded up, loaded into a trailer, and driven to the ferry terminal, he seemed to trust me and walked next to me up the ship's ramp onto the car deck. He was no problem at all. When we arrived in Freshwater there was a twenty-five mile walk home with him. Chief was so placid that he would have let me get on his back and hitch a lift. Meanwhile, Roger hadn't known what my intentions were, but he seemed resigned to the fact that I was wilful and a little bit bonkers.

Never having owned a horse, let alone broken one in, a book from the library was my next acquisition. Following that book to the letter seemed like the best thing to do. The book said that it takes six weeks to do it properly and it wasn't wrong. That is exactly how long it took.

I had befriended a man named Frank who was ninety-plus years old. I started going to have tea with him regularly. However, after seeing his cat on the table drinking milk from the top of the milk bottle, I politely declined the offer of a cuppa after that. I took him stews and cakes and enjoyed our chats. Frank gave me advice about how to break Chief in, cowboy style. Frank had emigrated to the USA with his wife in the late 19th century. He showed me a black-and-white photo of him and his wife in a covered wagon at the start of the goldrush. It was enthralling; it looked exactly like it was a scene from a cowboy movie. I later realized that Frank owned some small fields around the village, one of which he rented to me for Chief. At ten shillings a month, this was an exciting and unexpected bonus towards making my dream become a reality. Life really was good.

We had added to our family with another daughter, Louise, so it felt like our lives were complete, but then a further bout of the 'baby-blues' took my feet away from under me. With the added responsibility of being a new mother, I had to overcome it. Easier said than done!

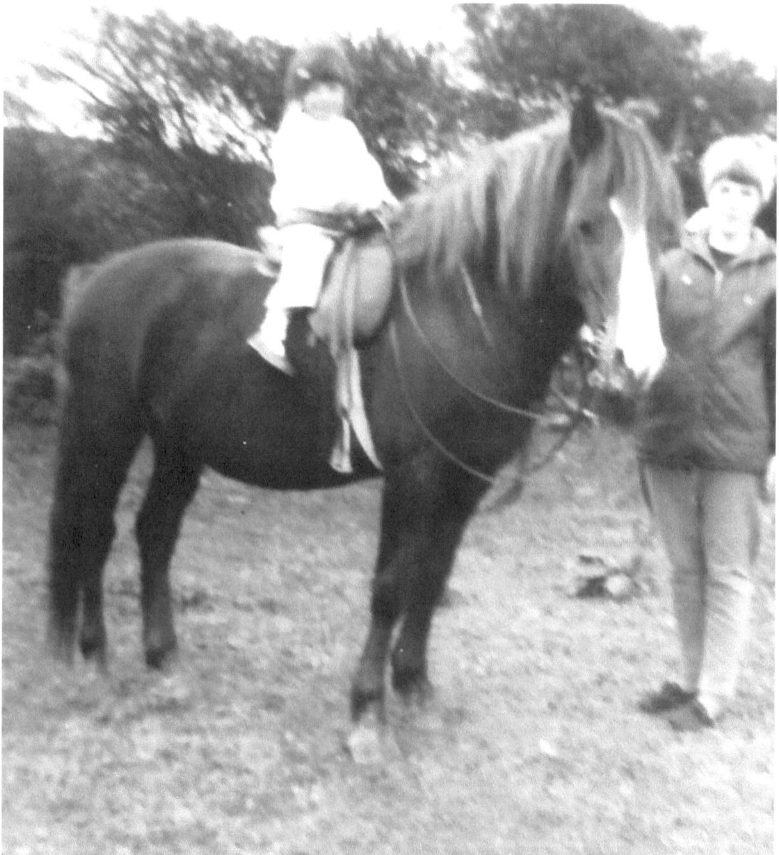

CHAPTER EIGHTEEN

STUMBLING AT THE FIRST FENCE

The halcyon days on the Isle of Wight didn't last. Roger's opinion of me had gone downhill. He kept telling me how disappointed he was with me as a wife. Our life and relationship just deteriorated. I didn't seem to be able to do anything right in his eyes.

I spent more time with my children and my pony. Roger kept losing his job, this led to a lack of respect from me towards him. It was me shoring up our finances all the time with part time jobs, plus I was breaking in horses and giving riding lessons. But things just got worse. Roger was a good father, just not a good husband. In his frustration, he turned the blame onto me, calling me a useless wife and mother, and telling me how disappointed he was with me. He used to give me £8 a week for housekeeping, then complained, by Monday that the fridge was empty. Roger decided from then on, he would do the shopping. This was an unrealistic idea.

By then I'd moved into the spare bedroom, which gave me some space. I was worn down by being constantly told what a useless woman and mother I had turned out to be. It was very easy for me to believe what he was saying; he was making me believe it to be true. Roger used to tell me to clear off once he was home. I would go around to various friends' houses for the evening, wait for the lights to go off, then creep home. It was my only option.

One evening I had had enough, along with my long-suffering friends. The next evening when Roger told me to f**k off out, I refused to be turned out again. Roger turned to Lorna and Lou and asked them if they would like to go with him to the fish and chip shop or stay here with 'this trollop'. You can guess what their innocent answer was. From that day on, I vowed never to allow him to use the girls against me again, nor me against them.

It was my mother's suggestion, to try to petition for a divorce on the grounds of mental cruelty and unreasonable behaviour. I employed the services of a solicitor on legal aid. Truly believing that Lorna and Louise would be better off without me, I packed my black Morris Minor in the middle of the night with my clothes and essentials and moved out the next day. Luckily for me, as I left to go to work next morning, never to return, no-one saw my tears.

My lawyer was compiling evidence (in those days you had to prove everything). I informed my lawyer that life had become intolerable for me and therefore I had left. He was furious because leaving the marital home, had weakened my case. He asked when I was going to see the children, to which I replied "I'm not. They're better off without me!" Picking up the phone he rang Roger to tell him to make the children available every Sunday at 2 pm. "Christine. will pick them up."

Afraid that they wouldn't want to see me or that they would kick and scream, a good idea crossed my mind—buy four fluffy yellow ducklings for them to name and take care of every Sunday, giving them something exciting to look forward to! As it happened, they loved the place where I lived, the horses, and the ducks but they especially loved the Wendy-house type caravan. These were happy times, albeit short. They looked forward to their visits, and that helped enormously to create and renew a mother and daughter bond away from home and relationship pressures.

I lived there from September to December, seeing Lorna and Lou each Sunday for the afternoon. After three lonely months, there was a tap on the door at 7 pm. To my delight, there were Lorna and Lou with two big boxes, one full of clothes, the other with toys. Roger had dumped them there and driven away, he had been evicted out of the bungalow through non-payment of the mortgage and a subsequent loan he took out using the property as security to buy himself a new car. They were here to stay. Life might have been tricky for a while, but it was also fun and a good bonding time. The three of us lived in the caravan until Easter when I got a job at Woodend with a flat.

During these months I acquired a job as groom to the Isle of Wight hunt master, mornings-only, six days a week. My new daily routine was muck out the stables on the farm where we lived, take Lorna and Lou to school, which was en-route to where the hunt master lived, do my job, and go home! It all fitted in well and gave me enough money to live on.

We lived in the caravan through the winter of 1974. I was on the council house waiting list, but in the spring, people were turned out of their temporary lets in holiday camps and, as I still had a roof over my head, I went further down the waiting list.

CHAPTER NINETEEN

Woodend Stud

Spring 1974, and a friend told me that she knew of a job working with horses, and there was a flat going with the job. I caught the ferry to Portsmouth and was picked up and taken for an interview. Miss Broad, the owner, seemed to think I would suit the job. I asked about wages, and she replied that if I was good, she'd pay eighteen pounds a week, otherwise, it was fifteen pounds. I accepted the job; and we moved over to Woodend at Easter.

The trees were just coming into leaf and the blossom was beginning to come out. It felt like a new start for us. Now the three of us were joined by our five-year-old Irish Setter, Honey, who my mother had been taking care of for me. Miss Broad insisted that my dog and children were not allowed to come down into the stable yard. Lorna was eight years old, and Lou was four at that time. One day Lou wandered down and was knocked over and bitten on her cheek by Miss Broad's two Doberman dogs. Miss Broad just said to us, "You were warned".

I worked for 3 weeks with no money. When I asked for my wages, she told me that she had decided to pay me eighteen pounds a week, but she would deduct three pounds per week for the flat. The flat was above the coach house. It was bare and basic, no furniture in the so-called sitting room, the double beds in the bedrooms had seen better days and probably many people had slept there. Because I had to take time out to take Lorna and Lou to school and back (she allowed me 1 hour in the morning and afternoon for this) my day started at 6 am to compensate.

The first job of the day was to ride the stallion out from 6am to 7.30am, then feed the horses while Lorna and Lou were in bed. I'd run upstairs to get Lorna and Lou up, give them breakfast, then it was off to school. Having six horses to ride every day for a minimum of one hour each, soon gave me a permanent blister on the base of my spine. To maximize my time and save money, I took Lorna and Lou to school on horseback; this got at least one horse exercised. At 3 pm it was time to go and collect the children and give them their tea. Then, I'd complete all the other stable duties until 6pm. Phew! This included going down to the farm to bring all the mares and foals in for the night.

While I did this task on my own, Miss Broad had the annoying habit of letting her Doberman dogs out of the van. They would immediately run off into the woods. She had no way of recalling them, so I would have to wait until they returned; never mind that time was ticking by and my children were waiting for their tea!

A local farm worker we called Mike the Bike befriended me. He always wore a woolly hat and had long scraggy hair, and terrible acne. However, he was a very kind young man and he used to bring me 56lb bags of potatoes from the farm. Every morning found me getting up at 5.45am, whizzing around all the sheds, barns, and stables, and collecting the bantam chicken eggs from wherever I could find them. The bantam chickens were semi-wild and often had chicks. There were a lot of feral cats about, too, with their sickly kittens in the hay barn.

Our staple diet was potatoes, mashed, boiled or roast with fried bantam eggs and baked beans. Money was so tight then that I would creep out in the dark to Miss Broad's wood store to help myself—well, to be honest, to steal logs for my fire. During the daytime I would sort out a few, small enough to fit on my fire, then I'd go back after dark to collect them. One night while in the store with an armful of logs Miss Broad came in with her Dobermans, which terrified me. Would the dogs smell me? Would she catch me? I listened to my heartbeat, pressing myself against the wall, thinking to myself, what's happened to me, that I'm reduced to doing this? Could I ever sink any lower? Being a twenty-six-year-old one-parent mother with two children, who will ever want me? I thought my life was over.

Taking Lou and Lorna off to school.
Riding there killed two birds with one stone!

CHAPTER TWENTY

Along came Richard.

While working at the Woodend stud, I was unexpectedly joined by two Swedish girls, Pia, and Lena, who moved into the flat! They were work experience girls on a summer break. I was a little bit angry that they were living in the flat that I was paying the rent on but I had no choice. The first thing that I knew about it was when Miss Broad introduced them to me and told me that they would be sleeping in the flat with me. Because the flat was subject to my working at Woodend, I just had to put up with it.

It helped my morale to have adult female company and we used to go to the pub one night a week together. One time, Pia and Lena met a group of young men who asked us out. The following weekend we went out with them, using my car because I didn't want to feel trapped. We all got on quite well. They seemed like decent young men, so we invited them into my flat for a drink and chat. Because there was very little furniture, we all sat on the floor. Inevitable, I ended up sitting next to one of them. His name was Richard, he was 5 years younger than me, was a bit plump, and had medium length hair and a full moustache. He was wearing a red and white check shirt with a wide leather belt and jeans, a bit like a wanabe cowboy! A stable girl named Margaret, who was too young to go to the pub with us, looked after Lorna and Lou for me.

They were instructed not to get out of bed that night, and in the event of meeting these young men, not to call me mother!

The following week arriving home from shopping I found Richard playing with Lorna and Lou in the stable yard. He had come to ask me out. I assumed that he would change his mind once he discovered that these two little girls were mine. None of it! I soon found out that he was a single dad with a three-year-old daughter. Richard was a farm worker living in a farm cottage about five miles away. He was twenty-one years old, and I was twenty-six.

He knew Mike the Bike, and knowing that, I gave Richard some credibility. Richard's wife had left him for an older man, leaving their daughter, Melanie, with Richard. Richard's mother looked after Melanie during the week and Richard had her at the farm at the weekend. He brought Melanie to Woodend to meet us. She was a very sweet little blonde girl with bright blue eyes. It wasn't long before Richard asked me to move in with him at Pitlands Farm. Seeing this as an escape from the 72-hour week that I was doing, was a no brainer for me; I seemed to have the mindset that the grass was definitely greener.

We moved into the Pitlands farm cottage at Up Marden. It was miles from anywhere, no shops; just a pub two miles down the road. Lorna and Louise enjoyed those years, playing around the farm with the children from the neighbouring farm, playing in the hay barn, and climbing on the tractors (I found this out a few years later).

I got a job working as a nursing auxiliary at St Richard's Hospital, in Chichester. They were very long hours, but I was quite happy in the knowledge that Lorna and Louise were picked up from the farm by a school minibus every morning and taken to school. Then they were brought home in the afternoon after school and Richard was working around the farmyard, so that was OK.

I came home from work one day to find that the girls hadn't been to school. This was very worrying so I telephoned the school liaison officer who said that the driver of twenty-five years' service had retired, and they couldn't find a replacement. So, I said, "What about me?" They told me to go in for a driving test and the job was mine. I earnt more money driving the bus 5 hours a day, 5 days a week with all the school holidays off, than I did nursing. I drove the school bus all around the outlying villages and farms, up roads not big enough for the main coaches. I did this job for 12 years until my accident at Woodend later.

CHAPTER TWENTY-ONE

THE HUNT MASTER
POPPING BACK IN TIME FOR A MOMENT

I worked for Jack Ellis, the hunt master, for two hunting seasons, and as a chalet maid in the summer, so it worked out very well indeed. However, life has an irritating habit of surprising you just when you think that you have experienced it all! During the second season Jack started stalking me, trapping me inside the tack room or stable and demanding a kiss for releasing me. Each time I fobbed him off, managing to slip out.

Unexpectedly he invited me to go to the annual hunt ball with him. Naïve or what? Incredibly, that flattered me! He picked me up from my house and we drove to the ballroom. However, he stopped at the bottom of the car park, saying that it wouldn't be so good for us to go in together. Dutifully getting out of the car as asked, I entered alone. What a shame that I was so stupid for not recognizing this as the bad sign that it was. A group of my hunting friends found this all very amusing and teased me. I begged them to take me home, but their answer was that it was strict etiquette to go home with the person who took you in the first place. Eventually they realised my fears were genuine and founded, so at the end of the ball, we went down to their car. We were very quickly followed by Jack calling my name.

In the end they persuaded me to go with him, swearing that they would follow. Jack set off. I couldn't see that they were behind us and very soon Jack backed into the entrance to a field saying he needed a pee. At that very moment, the headlights of my friends' car came on. Jack zoomed out at high speed and took me home although my friends lost us when they had to turn around in the field entrance. From then on life working for Jack was just embarrassing so I resigned.

So later, having left the Isle of Wight behind me, and having moved to Woodend in Sussex, imagine my shock on returning home from shopping to find Jack chatting with Miss. Broad! She mentioned how wonderful it was that Jack had come to visit and take me out to dinner. "He must think a lot about you to come all this way to take you out to dinner," she said.

He announced that he would pick me up at 7.30 pm, so 7 pm found me. putting a chair up against the door to the flat. Desperate measures: there was no lock on the door! I got into bed with Lorna and Lou, telling them we were going to play a game and pretend we weren't in. Sure enough, Jack arrived, he managed to push the door slightly ajar. He kept calling my name; it was so creepy, and my heart was pounding. Jack hung around for all of ninety minutes before giving up. The next morning, he reappeared and I verbally laid into him for frightening my children. I never saw him again.

CHAPTER TWENTY-TWO

Pride

Working Life

I had suffered an accident with one of Miss Broad's ponies, after which I considered that my leg was 'dodgy' I decided that it would be safer not to drive a minibus full of children. As I worked for the West Sussex County Council, they transferred me over to residential care work. This was a very good option and an introduction to a completely new area of work for me.

As a carer my first position was with people with learning difficulties in a brand-new halfway house designed to help to integrate people into the community. This home catered for twenty-four adults. Nine people from institutional mental hospitals soon arrived. They weren't mentally ill; they had arrived at their stations in life in Epsom where, through no fault of their own, they lived there for most of their lives, and now their home was being closed. They were soon followed by a young eighteen-year-old girl who was transferred from a children's home in East Sussex that was closing. Her loving mother was thrilled by this because it brought her closer to home at last. I'll call her Wendy here although this was not her real name. I was on duty at the time that Wendy arrived. No day care had been planned, so my task was to take care of Wendy for the day and take her to the park. We bonded.

After some time had passed, more residents arrived and therefore more staff were taken on. Wendy had complex needs. One day I arrived at work for an afternoon shift. My boss said, "Thank goodness you're here. Can you get Wendy out of the office?" Walking into the office I found Wendy sitting on the floor. She looked up at me and I simply said, "Come on, get up, come with me." She just stood up, took my hand and off we went. In hindsight, there's no doubt in my mind that other staff were jealous of the bond that we had. They did not appreciate how that bond had come about.

A promotional opportunity arrived when a Care Officer post was created. I applied.

At the interview I was asked, "Why do you think that Wendy does as you say?"

I replied in all honesty, "I have no idea, but my children, dogs and horses all do what I say; I never need to chastise them."

The promotion was mine. At the subsequent staff meeting, the manager told me that 'they' had been watching me and had concluded that when giving instructions or requests I always have a pan/po face, (expressionless) and because of this I never give mixed messages, keeping to the point, with few words.

During training, we were given this example.
  "John, go to your room and get your coat. We're going out on the bus!"
Ten minutes later, where is John?
All John heard was "go to your room."
Sure, enough there he is sitting on his bed!
The staff were all subsequently told to follow my example.

After ten years in this post, I was due for a change of scene. Transferring to an adult elderly residential care presented me with a totally different way of working. This home was a small unit of nine residents with dementia. One of the gentlemen there used to shout. One evening, the night staff said that he was disturbing the other residents. The solution was a simple one; I entered his room, and said, "Shhhh, you'll wake the baby." Immediately he agreed to be quiet and went to sleep.
  Whilst working as Team Leader it was a requirement to take the NVQ (National Vocational Qualification) in management. The first thing I had to do was to have lessons in how to use a computer. West Sussex County council were upgrading all their systems. For someone

'without an academic brain cell in my head' this was quiet daunting. It took me two years to complete this qualification in my spare time, with monthly tutorials. I was told that with this qualification, NVQ level 4 in Management, I could get a job as manager in childcare, learning difficulties or senior care. I was very proud, having been described in my early years as 'a dead-end kid, going nowhere'. Additionally, it was necessary for me to become an NVQ assessor in order to have a fully qualified work team, with all the care staff qualified. I felt valued and valuable to my workplace.

I carried on with this career for another fifteen years, both as a day team leader and a night team leader until my retirement at the age of sixty.

CHAPTER TWENTY-THREE

Pride in my ponies

Having had a selection of ponies while I lived on the IOW, during those years I learned a great deal about the care of them. Sadly, through circumstances at those times, I had to sell or give all my ponies away, all except Alpha who was in foal with Robin, Later on when I was more settled, Alpha and her foal were brought over to Woodend, Miss Broad had consented to them coming and being put in with her mares and foals.

Once I had begun carriage driving I became very proud of my driving ponies; their welfare was paramount to me. They had to be properly prepared for the work that was going to be asked of them. Keeping them very fit, healthy and happy was the key. To maintain this mantra, it was my duty to have a routine and stick to it, to vary their fitness training to keep their minds and bodies in top form. Achieving this filled me with pride.

My daughters used to ride them up on the downs once a week, galloping flat out to give them a blast; this helped to maintain the ponies' strong lungs. On hot days we took the ponies to the beach to swim with them. This helped to strengthen their muscles at the same time as saving their legs and feet from pounding the roads. It was also a treat for the young girls who used to come to the stables to help me.

My daily routine was up at six am, drive to the stables using the school minibus, to give the ponies their breakfast. The swimming pool opened at seven am, and my aim was to be the first person in the pool every morning. Then it was half-an-hour swimming, followed by a shower. Eight am saw me collect my lady escort from her home (because on my bus there were young vulnerable children, some with learning difficulties, which made it essential to always have an escort). Eight thirty am until nine thirty was the school run, picking up from the farms and villages and driving to various schools in Chichester. Then it was back to drop off my escort. Nine thirty, and it was back to the stables, to muck out and brush the ponies. Exercising them, in a variety of ways including driving them up the downs, kept them fresh and interested. Sometimes I would do some dressage training in the field. Then it was time to feed the ponies their lunch. One pm saw me driving home to do some housework and prepare supper. At three pm it was back to collect my escort and on to collect the children from school to take them home, drop off my escort, and back to the stables to feed the ponies at five pm. Next, I would go back home to get dinner ready, and finally ten pm saw me off to the stables to feed the ponies and clean out any muck. This routine never varied. The key was to feed the ponies little and often, never too much food in one meal, otherwise their bodies could not metabolize it enough. The ponies thrived on continuity and routine.

CHAPTER TWENTY-FOUR

BACK ON THE FARM

Having moved into the farm cottage with Richard, it was easy for me to concentrate on training Alpha to be driven. The farm was in the middle of nowhere surrounded by country lanes, with virtually no traffic, so it was easy to drive Alpha around. It was hilly, so she got quite fit. My farrier on the Isle of Wight built me a lovely little buggy. Lorna and Lou used to come out with me, and our dog Gemma ran behind.

Gemma was a fabulous border collie that we got from the shepherd on the next-door farm. We were given her when she was just six weeks old; she had been weaned onto bread soaked in milk, Odd! She nearly bit my finger when I gave her a piece of chicken for the first time. Gemma was incredibly easy to train, as if she was born obedient. Once gemma joined the family, she came everywhere with us, including travelling in the lorry to compete around the UK.

After joining a local harness club, I found out that they were running a competition, a one-day event with dressage, a short cross country, and cones. There was no question about it, I entered the event with Alpha, driving her in the buggy that was made for me by my farrier. Dressage, marathon, and cones is the format for national competitions. Winning this local and low-key competition. HOOKED me into the world of National carriage driving competitions.

Richard and his friend built me a four wheeled vehicle for two ponies. The style of carriage that he built was like a wagonette; it had four wheels and a central pole designed for a pair of ponies to drive. Now that Robin had come of age, I trained him to ride and drive, so we put Alpha and Robin together in the home-built wagon and entered the national driving event at Cricket St Thomas in Somerset (where 'to the manor born' was filmed) This was an event that, if I won, would qualify me for the national driving Championships at Osberton, Northamptonshire later in the year.

Being early in the year, the ground was soggy, and there was a steep hill that we had to climb. There were two abandoned vehicles at the bottom of the hill that had failed to get up it, so the drivers had withdrawn. Despite being twenty minutes late to finish the marathon, I discovered that I was the first competitor to complete the course. The course designer rushed over on his quad bike to see if we were OK. I won the event and found myself crying like a baby at what my ponies had done for me when I was presented with the trophy. All within one year, I had won my only event and qualified for the national championships.

CHAPTER TWENTY-FIVE

BRIGHTON DRIVING TRIALS

My First Encounter with The Press!

The following season started at an event in Stanmer Park near Brighton. It was quite a challenging event, very hilly, and the ponies were naturally not competition fit, so I'm very proud to say that we won it.

Afterwards, having just won the event, while I was waiting outside the arena to go in to be presented with my winner's cup a couple walked up to me. They claimed to be from the newspapers and were writing about local people who had tasted success in their life, and they had been directed to me. They assumed that I was quite well off and said so! My reply was, "No! Don't be daft! You don't need to be rich to do well at this sport. These were my children's ponies, the carriage has been built by my husband, and we are now living in a council house. The harness is a mishmash of two single sets converted for a pair and our lorry was loaned to us by a friend. Money cannot guarantee you success."

The following week, a double-spread article was in the evening Argos newspaper. The headline was,

'Council Tenants Shine at Royal Sport.'

A quote from me was,

'You don't need to be rich to do well at this sport.'

Cringe!

CHAPTER TWENTY-SIX

Stepping back in time

My First Accident

In 1978, I no longer lived at Woodend. Having moved into the Pitlands farm cottage with Richard, I was still working mornings over at Woodend with the ponies there. I owed Miss Broad £20 pounds for some hay, and she contacted me asking if I was willing to work the debt off by going over and driving Fruky. She added that he needed my attention.

As soon as his harness was on him, my trained eye knew that something serious had happened; the brass turrets that the reins run through on his back were squashed flat. Something serious must have happened; he must have reared up and come over onto his back whilst in harness. Miss Broad insisted that this was not so; no-one but I had handled him. I should have listened to my instincts! Not long afterwards someone told me that one of Miss Broad's many Swedish stable girls had come into the yard with grazed forearms and had quit the very next day!

Despite my misgivings we drove Fruky, and it very soon became apparent that something had indeed happened. He was very nervous and suddenly spooked by a car coming towards us. He lunged for the bushes. At my insistence we drove him into a field away from any traffic, but when he saw the top of a car above the hedgerow he instantly took off, bolting at a gallop! This was an emergency. I quickly decided to drive him directly into a very thick hedgerow to stop him, as by now he was in a flat-out gallop. But suddenly Miss Broad panicked and grabbed the reins from me. By doing so she inadvertently flipped the carriage onto its side, throwing me and her out on the ground. Fruky galloped across a road with the carriage still on its side. A tractor driver saw him attempt to jump a barbed wire fence, which brought him to an abrupt halt. Miraculously Miss Broad was unharmed and so was Fruky; however, Fruky was turned out into a field and was never driven again.

The tractor driver came looking for us and found Miss Broad laying there unconscious and me trying to get up, but my right leg wouldn't work. He called 999 and an ambulance took us to St Richard's Hospital in Chichester. After an X-Ray, the doctor informed me that I had sustained a broken hip and needed an operation.

I had a lifelong fear of hospitals, resulting in me having both my children at home. Oh, my goodness! It was a terrifyingly frightening prospect! The anaesthetist came to see me and asked if I had any questions. I told him I was afraid of dying on the operating table. He assured me that he would take good care of me and gave me a pre-med injection. The next thing I knew, I was back on the ward, it was done. That was a revelation to me, realizing that if I had died, I wouldn't have known a thing about it while others would mourn me. This subsequently helped me later in life. I realised that times come when it is the right moment to say goodbye to some of my animals, leaving me to grieve while they sleep in their eternal peace.

Next day, the surgeon came to check on me and asked me if I had fallen off a horse.

"No, I fell out of a carriage," I replied.

From then I was known as the woman who did what HRH Prince Philip did.

It was after this accident that I gave up driving the school bus, and started my new career as a carer.

CHAPTER TWENTY-SEVEN

My Second Accident

A year after my first accident I asked for the screws to be removed from my hip. I had that operation, and at the moment of discharge from hospital I was told to 'go and do what you do'. That was a green light for me to start driving again.

Bearing in mind that Alpha was getting older, I had been looking for a replacement. One of my customers who I taught to drive, offered to buy me one of my choosing, and he would finance it.

I found a good-looking pony and had successfully trained it to drive. The local harness club were running a one-day event up at Goodwood (my home territory) and I decided to use this event as a training exercise. The new pony was paired up with Robin and I entered the one-day event that was held up next to Goodwood racecourse. My mind wasn't fully on the job, and I spent too much time chatting with fellow drivers. Aged 16, Lorna was going to be my groom, standing on the back of the carriage. We set off on the marathon heading down a hill towards

Singleton. The hill got steeper and steeper, and the ground was wet and slippery chalk. I soon realized that we were going too fast to make a safe right-hand turn. So, we hung on for dear life out of control. I was later told by a man who realised that I was in trouble that he ran down the hill after me and saw huge stretches where the carriage had left the ground; there were no skid marks for several metres. I knew we were heading for a large village pond, but I had no idea how deep it was! I had read in the newspapers that a team of four horses in the USA had struck out into a small lake until they were out of their depth and the carriage, they were pulling dragged them under, drowning them all. With this in my mind I chose to drive into a nearby tree, but a large rock flipped us over. As soon as I hit the deck, I knew that my leg was broken. Someone managed to catch my ponies unharmed. Robin was traumatised. The new pony was never driven again. Rest and recuperation for Robin and re-uniting him with his mother help enormously for his future in carriage driving once I had recovered.

At the time of the accident, although un-hurt, Lorna was very distressed. She partly blamed herself because she had argued with Richard over being on the back of the carriage. She thought he would have had more strength to stop the whole process. That was not the case. It was a chain of circumstances that had led to this tragedy.

This time when the ambulance arrived, they asked me if I had fallen off a horse. When I said no, I had fallen out of a carriage, they playfully quipped,

"That's funny we had a lady last year who did the same thing."

I cried out in pain, "that was me!"

They later told me that they were going to put on the side of the ambulance, 'By Royal Appointment'. I had never experienced such pain or embarrassment before in my life.

CHAPTER TWENTY-EIGHT

THE ROAD TO RECOVERY

This was the beginning of a few years of surgery for me. After my second driving accident where my thighbone had shattered through the screw holes, the surgeon inserted a Zickel nail right down the inside of my thigh bone. That meant that my right leg had a new alignment which made it difficult for me to walk and climb up onto the carriage.

After a couple of years, the surgeon who treated me refused to remove it, saying he had never done it before and feared that the femur would break. I asked for a second opinion and was sent to St. Thomas' Hospital in London. There I saw Mr. Heatly, who said that the Zickel nail would have to be removed at some point because it was inevitable that I would have to have a hip replacement. He said that he had already taken five out and would do it for me. So, I went into St Thomas' Hospital, London, and had it removed.

Everything was fine for about six weeks but then suddenly I found myself in a lot of pain. Mr. Heatly told me that he was not surprised in the least, and that the socket had collapsed. He asked me if I would attend a conference, because St. Thomas's is a teaching hospital; my age and my situation were of particular interest for the young doctors to study and learn from.

I went to the conference and had to lay on a bed with a huge mirror angled above it so that the students could easily observe me. A senior consultant sitting at the front row told Mr. Heatly that he would not touch me with a bargepole unless I gave up my equestrian pursuits. Mr. Heatly replied tartly, "We are talking quality of life and Christine is rather good at it." Upon looking at all the options it was decided that Mr. Heatly would put in a very new style of hip replacement.

"I have a man up there who has the very first uncemented hip replacement, so let us see how he gets on, then I will do yours," he told me.

Through annual check-ups, I grew to respect and admire Mr. Heatley. One day he told me that as a 'professor' he no longer did his check-ups! However, that was the day he told me that it was his 'protégé, Mr. Nunn, who had performed my surgery under his watchful eye. Mr. Nunn is now senior consultant at 'Guys,' the sister hospital of St Thomas, Mr. Heatly recommended that I be transferred over to Mr. Nunn's care. I have had this new artificial hip now for thirty-five years.

CHAPTER TWENTY-NINE

FOSTERING

During this time Richard and I decided that we wanted to give something back to help disadvantaged children, so we started to do fostering. It involved a lot of training, so that it took nearly a year before we were registered. **Finally,** we were accepted. Soon I had a phone call asking if we could take in a teenager, and with Richard's agreement the answer was, yes. That afternoon Gareth arrived with his social worker and a plastic bag of his belongings. He moved in and was immediately at home and comfortable, commandeering the sofa and the TV remote control!

Aged 16, Lou was working at Goodwood airfield as an office junior and was still living at home. She was not keen that Gary called me Mum. Gary was part of the family for 3 years. For a short time, (between) Gary came with us to competitions at home and abroad.

There were times when I was unable to work because of my hip socket's collapse, I was in a lot of pain and took strong pain killers. I wasn't getting up early and doing very little during the day except watch TV. I became aware that Gary was coming into my bedroom in the morning and looking at me. I was a bit worried about it, so I told his social worker, Colin. Colin collected Gary from school that day and took him to Burger King for a casual chat. It transpired that Gary was very worried about me and wanted to check that I was still alive before he went to school.

I was still going to driving events. I bought myself a comfortable garden reclining chair to sit in at the competitions to rest my back and leg. My friend Angie used to grab it for herself, so I told Gary to sit in it and not let her have it. She simply tipped him out.

After Gary left school, he worked in my husband's garage, Richard had gone into business with his friend Mike, and they were doing very well. Gary loved to tinker with anything mechanical. At the age of eighteen, Gary no longer came under the care of Social Services and moved out of our house. Unfortunately, my marriage to Richard failed. Working for Richard, Gary was privy to this situation and came to offer me his support. After that we lost touch with each other, but recently we were re-united and are now firm friends.

THE DUKE OF EDINBURGH AND I

CHAPTER THIRTY

NATIONAL COMPETITIONS

Realizing that I could no longer compete at national level with our home-built wagon, Richard and I decided to invest in a Bennington Phaeton, a rather swanky carriage with a royal heritage. We sold the wagonette to Miss Broad for use in continuing to break her ponies in to drive, to make them more saleable.

Richard had started a car repair and sales business in partnership with our friend, Mick Adair, in a garage on the industrial estate in Chichester, and it was doing very well. We bought our own lorry.

It was a bit of a wreck. Richard refurbished it with a new body and configured the inside to suit our needs, installing an electric winch to pull our carriages (by then we had 2, one for dressage, the other for cross-country) up the ramp, and designing the new interior so that we could have compartments for the pair of ponies to sleep in. He also added a side awning so that we could store the carriages under cover at events and adapted the interior as a tack room and horse food store. The ponies were stabled inside.

I competed with the help of my family at Windsor Park, Sandringham, Scone Palace twice, Kelso Racecourse, Brighton three years running, Tatten Park, Osberton, Harrogate, Wyly, and Cricket St Thomas for three years, winning each year. We also won at Castle Howard. During this time Gary was still with us and he was very useful to have around. He helped wherever he could, cleaning carriages and harness, grooming the ponies, and so on. He also came out with me on the backstep of the carriage when I was exercising them.

We tried to do two competitions on one round trip to save fuel. As mentioned earlier, we made many friends during these driving years and went to all the competitors' party nights. We were never out of the first three. However, the title of National Champion eluded me.

*Robin and Alpha at Cricket St Thomas
in our home-built wagon.*

The Water Hazard, Windsor Great Park, National Championships

CHAPTER THIRTY-ONE

DEVELOPMENTS AND DR. SNOW

In 1981 an Australian Equestrian researcher came to England to work with the British driving society, Federation Equestrian International (FEI) to monitor the stress levels of competing horses. Dr Snow had already worked with the horse event fraternity and racehorses but had never had the opportunity to work with ponies.

After my accidents and a forced break from competing. I took the opportunity to buy a 3-year-old pony from a stud farm. She had the best of temperaments, and was very laid back; nothing phased her. I called her Siggy. I brought her on gently. At the age of 5 years old, she stepped into the limelight with Robin at national competitions.

My ponies were chosen to take part in Dr. Snow's research. The first event of the season was always at Brighton and at 6 am on marathon day, a vet's assistant took some blood samples. At the same time Robin and Siggy were fitted with heart monitors. Brighton marathons were very hard with a lot of steep hills. The marathon consisted of five sections: roads, and tracks, usually eight kilometres at fourteen kph followed by a one kilometre walk at six kph, with a ten-minute rest period with a vet check.

Section three was a short sharp speed-trot, sixteen kph for five kilometres, and a second walk section with another rest period and vet check. Then the fun got going with the hazard/obstacle section, where there were eight obstacles to be negotiated at speed. Most spectators gathered at the water hazard. The ponies were checked at compulsory rest times (fitness was measured by the speed of recovery). At the end of the marathon more blood was taken. The research team showed me the printout of the heart monitor, which was frankly amazing. You could read it like a book; it showed the hills and the hazards with steep spikes that were followed by flat lines.

Dr Snow congratulated me on the welfare and fitness of my ponies, and this made me immensely proud. Only I knew the true extent of the performance of my ponies during a marathon; they had total trust in me. I often said they would drive over Beachy Head if I asked them to. To 'ask' was also the key to success, not to order, bully or force.

When being presented with a trophy, it was always a very proud moment for me, knowing that the 'team' that worked with me, my husband, daughters, girl grooms and helpers had done the very best, and the ponies had made me feel very proud. After the marathon was completed, the ponies had a good wash down, then were taken on a long rein to have a roll in the grass and eat some green fresh grass.

My mantra was, "It's us, competing against the course; whoever completes the three phases of the event best will be the winner." It never occurred to me that we were competing against other carriage drivers. I worked hard to improve my dressage with the plan in mind that if I scored well in the dressage arena, it could put me in the lead with a decent margin. We would be able to drive the marathon with a little more care. Knowing that, enabled me to have a different outlook on the marathons. No need for a make-or-break approach.

These events would take place over three to four days and after each phase all of us pony contestants and colleagues would relax together. There were different categories:

single pony, single horse,
pony pair, horse pair,
pony team of four,
horse team of four – this is the category that was considered the most elite.

HRH Prince Philip excelled in this last class and was a highly respected driver, especially bearing in mind his very full royal duties; it must have made it difficult to hone his skills. He was a very knowledgeable and skilled horseman.

Prince Philip was instrumental in the creation of the FEI rules.

CHAPTER THIRTY-TWO

FUN AT THE END OF THE DAY

In the evenings we would gather around a camp fire, usually sparked up by one of the drivers in the pony pair cate gory, and we would talk about the day and play jokes on each other.

A favourite joke was called 'airplanes'. We would get six people (girl grooms and helpers) and sit them in six chairs in a row of two by two. Five of the people knew the game and were prepared for it. They had to pretend that they were in an airplane with all the motions of a flight, we would all make a noise like the plane engines, then someone would shout, "the starboard engine's on fire!" and the person in the designated seat position had a bucket of water thrown over them. All in good fun.

We were a group of enthusiasts. I usually found myself in the top three in any competitive event, but there was no rivalry amongst us. If we didn't win, it was the course that beat us, not a fellow competitor.

When we were not competing, for a change of scene, we frequently took the ponies in the lorry to stay a weekend with a fellow carriage driver. The family always came with us, including Gareth.

CHAPTER THIRTY-THREE

ETON COLLAGE AND THE FILM PREMIER

HRH Prince Philip wrote a very informative and comprehensive book entitled.

Competition Carriage Driving

It was accompanied by a documentary film of the same name. All of the carriage drivers received an embossed invitation to attend the premier of the film which was held at Eton College film studio. Copies of Prince Philip's book were on sale there, and I bought one.

All the drivers sat in the small film studio at Eton Collage to watch the film, and Prince Philip sat amongst us.

There is a short sequence in the film where I can be seen driving through the spring blossom at Brighton driving trials. To say the very least, I felt privileged to be a part of this occasion when all the pony pair drivers got together.

CHAPTER THIRTY-FOUR

THE DUKE OF EDINBURGH AND I

My dear friend, Claudia Bunn, came to visit me in my hospital bed after my second accident. She was a formidable woman, with whom you did not argue. Claudia announced that, because of the trauma Lorna went through, she was going to take her back to her home, a farm on the English-Welsh border. Claudia drove a team of white ponies which involved a lot of hard work. Lorna was a great help with her ponies and went to several driving events with Claudia. At one of these events Lorna met Russell.

Russell worked for HRH Prince Philip as a junior groom. With the help of Claudia and Russell, Lorna got a job as stable girl to Peter Munt. Peter was a well-known coach driver who also competed at the driving trials and was also a friend of Prince Philip. Peter lived on the crown estate at Windsor and had the use of a stable yard on Windsor Park Estate. I assume that Peter and Prince Philip drove around the estate together.

Peter's wife, Ann, was a very elegant woman, tall and slim with blonde hair that she always wore up neatly in a group of curls. Ann was a movie stunt rider. She discovered that Lorna was a good cook and often asked Lorna if she would go in the kitchen and cook things such as spaghetti Bolognese for her and Peter. On a few occasions Prince Philip would knock on the door and come in, making himself at home in the kitchen. Lorna would promptly and politely leave.

Lorna went with Russell to the royal staff's Christmas Ball, held at Windsor Castle (on alternate years it was held at Buckingham Palace). Lorna told me afterwards that nearly all the royal family had come to welcome their staff but did not stay too long.

It was through this connection that I discovered that HRH Prince Philip had given signed copies of his book to his driving staff. This knowledge is what prompted me to ask him to sign my copy. I competed all over the UK and Scotland, and it was at an event at Scone Palace, when early one morning I went out to feed my ponies, and accidently bumped into Prince Philip, who was wandering around the stable yard enjoying the peace and quiet. That's when I cheekily asked if he would sign my copy of his book. He looked me up and down and said,

"I don't know you!"

When I told him that I was a fellow carriage driver he replied,

"OK, hurry up, and don't tell anyone."

While I was competing at Scone Palace, Lorna and Russell were walking along a track next to the River Tay when they saw Prince Philip laying on the bank in the long grass. He told them to go away because he didn't want to be disturbed, so they kept walking. Further along the track Prince Philip drove his Range Rover up next to them, and said, "Hop in, you two," and then drove them to his caravan and told them that they could help themselves to anything they fancied in the fridge. It was the last day, and it would all otherwise be thrown away.

A few years later, we had a flood in our house, and my precious book got water damaged. I eventually bought a copy of the second edition, but this had a different cover and was in landscape format. At the time I was giving my granddaughter, Fleur, lessons with the now 'old' Robin. I decided to send both books to Prince Philip with a covering letter explaining what had happened and saying that I hoped Fleur would follow in my carriage-driving footsteps. Within the week both books were returned to me with a covering letter. This time the prince had written 'Philip 2000' I feel very sure that this book is unique, I treasure both a lot.

There was an occasion when I was standing at the side of the arena watching the horse teams of four parading around. Prince Philip came and stood next to me. Hearing the thundering sound of these huge hooves as they passed by, I remembered my own accident. I shuddered and remarked to Prince Philip,

"Imagine being run away with, by these huge horses."

He turned to me and said, "It makes no difference, Shetland ponies or shire horses. In flight they are the same and cannot easily be stopped."

Wise words indeed.

Carriage driving is a very family orientated sport. All the family came and that included the dog. On one such occasion, going out for the day, to spectate at the Royal Windsor horse show, especially for the marathon of the horse driving three-day event, there was a gathering of spectators waiting for the appearance of Prince Philip's team. I then realized that a few metres away the Queen stood, very noticeably dressed in her traditional apparel of mackintosh, galoshes, and head scarf. She was accompanied by some of her grandchildren. Her majesty soon got excited, and I overheard the Queen saying to the grandchildren, "Grandpa's coming, Grandpa's coming." What a delightful family scene this was!

At every competition there was a marquee where people would eat and drink coffee with each other, The Duke would occasionally pop in. He showed a keen interest in all the other categories of drivers, often watching as we drove the hazards. Saturday evenings after the day's marathon sections, there would be a competitors' party. There would be a dance floor, and everyone would be happy and relieved that the day had gone smoothly with no mishaps or accidents.

During these evenings, Prince Philip would arrive and join in. As mentioned, carriage driving is very much a family sport, Competitors' children would be at the party, giving it a very wholesome atmosphere. I remember with fondness, doing the birdy song in a circle with Prince Philip joining in, and later we were all sitting on the floor with our legs linked with the person sitting in front of us to sing the *Rowboat song, 'Row Row Row the Boat, Merrily Down the Stream,'* then gathering in a circle to do the *'Okey Cokey'*. After all the merriment, Prince Philip would often waltz cheek-to-cheek with my friend, Ann Munt. It was a wonderful time in my life.

On an occasion when I was competing, Prince Philip spotted us with our Bennington Phaeton, the same make of carriage that he had, Prince Philip came over to chat with us about it and how we liked it.

Surrounded by press photographers, we were bombarded by.

"What did the Duke say?"

Our answer was, "It was just chit chat."

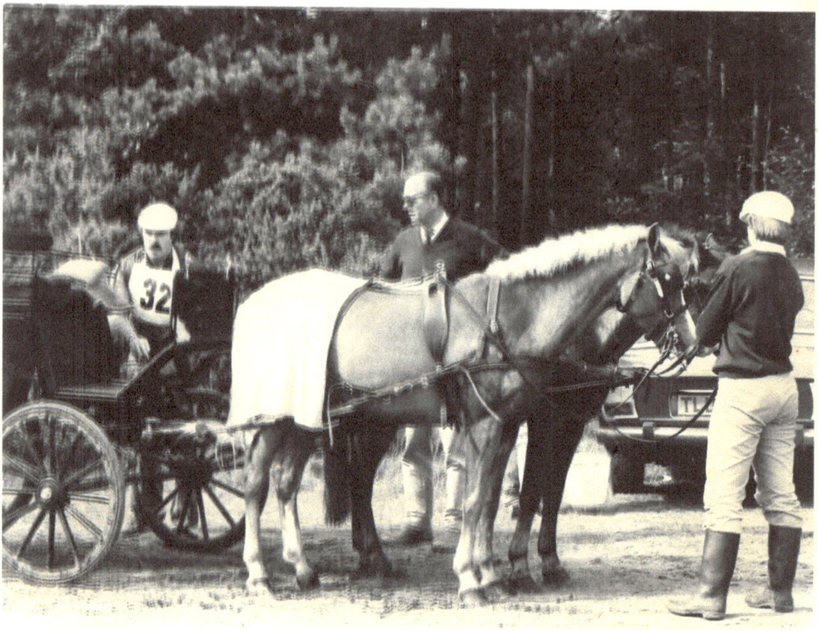
32

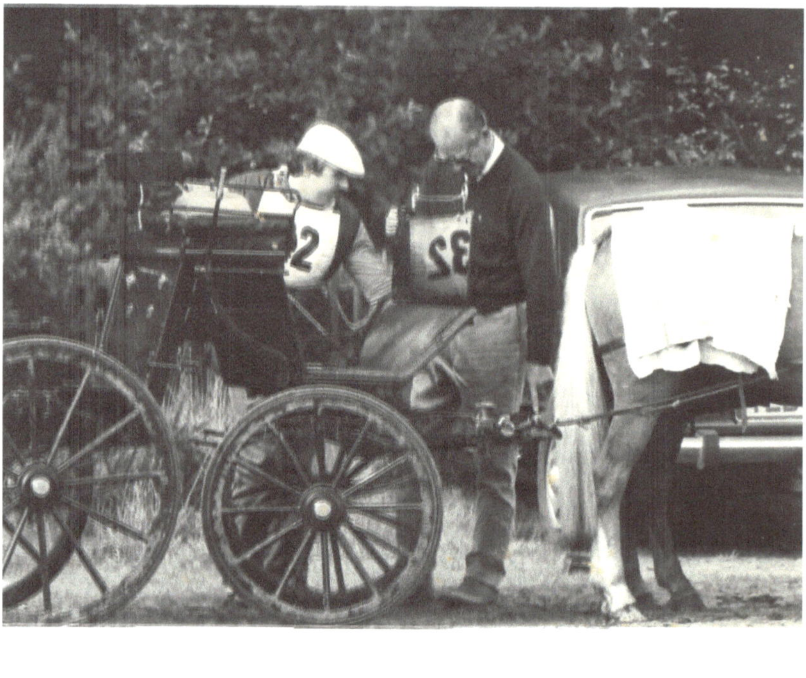
32

CHAPTER THIRTY-FIVE

WINDSOR, WEMBLEY, AND THE PITNEY-BOWES

Pitney Bowes pony pair championship was held on a Thursday in the summer months at Windsor Great Park. The top seven competitors went on to the International Horse Show at Wembley on the following Saturday evening to compete in a run-off of the cones section of the event. The cones course was a replica of the one at Winsor Park.

The competitors were allowed to walk the course to familiarize themselves at exactly 10 am in the morning; the cones were set up for exactly thirty minutes. On this occasion, somehow, we failed to go up to walk the course. The draw was done out of a hat for the running order, and I was hoping to be able to watch one of the other competitors do it before me. But, Oh my gosh! There I was—drawn first to go. I was led into the dark tunnel ready to enter the arena. In front of me was a huge blue curtain. Suddenly the curtain opened, the loudspeaker announced the Pitney Bowes Pair Championship was open, and some bright spark whacked my pony on his rump, thus catapulting me into the bright glare of the main arena. I had a quick look around and off we jolly well went with a reasonable time and no faults. The loudspeakers announced that I was the one to beat and I stayed in the lead until there were only two more to go.

The final two competitors were scurry drivers who had gate- crashed the event at Windsor knowing that the prize money of £250 would be easily won at Wembley because scurry driving is fast and furious, and the scurry drivers were very skilled at that. Wow! We ended up placed third overall, and a small clip of us was televised on the 'News at 10'.

Wembley Arena. Royal International Horse Show

CHAPTER THIRTY-SIX

HEW GRAHAM, SEEKING SPONSORSHIP.

I was meeting a local journalist, Hew Graham, to ask him if he could get me sponsorship, feeling that I had gone as far as I could with my current budget. He arranged a photo shoot with the ponies swimming in the sea off Selsey Beach. He was very enthusiastic about this, carrying out a very successful photo shoot, and he was thrilled with some of the photos.

Disaster struck the next day when my accident happened at Woodend. I telephoned him from my hospital bed to tell him that it was all over! "Nonsense," he said, "We can turn this to our advantage." At 9 pm that night he arrived at my hospital bed, telling me that he had arranged with the ward matron, for me and my bed to be taken down to the ground floor which would allow my ponies to be brought to see me through the open window. My response? NO WAY. What a load of unbelievable and embarrassing rubbish had got into Hew's brain? Instead, like most wise decisions in life, we arrived at a compromise. A few weeks later, I dressed up in my driving outfit, posing with my ponies. I found this all a bit tacky, to say the least.

Eventually, I was discharged home, and a letter dropped on my doormat. The envelope was embossed with the address, Buckingham Palace. Oh, my word! This was unbelievable! It was a letter from Prince Philip wishing me a speedy recovery. I wrote back thanking him, which prompted another letter from him. I was chuffed to bits by the fact that Prince Philip had written to me.

I told Hew about it. He phoned the next day to say that he had sold my story to a national newspaper. He told me that they would telephone me for an interview and that I should NOT talk to anyone else in the meantime. Sure enough, the phone kept ringing. After talking to the allotted national newspaper, incredibly, Hew rang to say he had now sold it for more money to a Sunday broadsheet.

"For goodness' sake Hew! I've already spoken to the newspaper." He said, "No worries, I've already been paid!"

Sure enough, this newspaper telephoned me for a chat as well, and asked if they could talk to Richard. Richard was at work, but he was allowed to take the call, during which one of his fellow workers called out his name, 'Dick.' Sure, as eggs are eggs, the following Sunday there it was:

'Dick and Phil: One lives in a council house the other in a palace, but nevertheless they're drinking buddies.'

What utter rubbish it was. Despite all this publicity, I never did get any sponsorship. I was so embarrassed. I could barely hold my head up at the competitions after that. Lucky for me, these experiences have resulted in me taking everything I read in the newspapers with a pinch of salt. It made me aware that the royal household must be inundated with false claims of one thing or another! From then onwards I never believed anything that appeared in the newspapers.

CHAPTER THIRTY-SEVEN

THE ANNUAL CONFERENCE AND DR. SNOW'S RESEARCH RESULTS

All the carriage drivers met up every autumn at an annual conference. It was an important event on the calendar when new committee members were chosen, events analysed, and new locations for events were discussed. It was a place to meet up and be seen. It would be held at a hotel with a conference room somewhere in the centre of the UK to enable as many drivers as possible to attend, usually, Hinckley, Leicestershire.

At this conference Dr Snow was a guest speaker. He had come to report his research findings, which proved consistently that the off-side animal (pony or horse) worked harder than the near-side one in carriage driving, and this was proved through heart monitor readings. This was very true of Robin and Siggy's heart monitor readings. Siggy was the off-side pony, and her heart rate was higher than Robin's. His heart rate peaked at two hundred and twenty beats per minute whereas Siggy's was two hundred and twenty-six beats per minute. A horse's heart explodes at two hundred and fifty beats per minute. The vital thing is the recovery rate and these peaks only lasted three to four seconds.

The Duke of Edinburg always attended the annual conferences, clearly feeling very comfortable. He was seen laughing and joking with other team drivers, no doubt sharing stories. It was always very apparent that the Duke enjoyed these times off from his royal duties; valuable time for him to relax and enjoy the company of like-minded people.

CHAPTER THIRTY-EIGHT

INTERNATIONAL COMPETITIONS

I had often expressed the idea of competing abroad; this would be the icing on the cake for me. To be allowed to do this we had to be given permission by the committee of the horse driving trials (HDT). Thrilling news came when they sent their approval.

I was the first person to represent Great Britain abroad, competing with ponies. As a Sussex girl it was featured on the BBC '*South Today*' programme which followed the BBC early evening news. A film crew came out to film me training in a river and the interviewer sat up next to me on the carriage while we drove back to the stables. He asked me why I still competed after having such a bad accident. Smiling coyly at him, I told him that it's simply a very consuming sport that the whole family could join in. It gave us a four-minute slot on the TV.

The first event in France was in Compiegne, north of Paris. In England, much as I loved going to all the National events, the entry fee was £50 and there was no prize money to be had. It was most definitely done for the love of carriage driving, and a social occasion for the whole family. Things equestrian abroad were just the opposite. We were paid £250 appearance money, given free stabling, and if we wanted to stay in a hotel that was included, too. However, I preferred to sleep very close to my ponies. We attended a gala dinner, won lots of trophies, prizes as well as bottles of French wine by the case, a driving whip and an old coach driving print, but most of all I enjoyed the prestige.

Later that year we went to compete in Waregem in Flanders, Belgium. Again, we had appearance money and lots of prizes. This time we were accompanied by Jill and Derek, another pony pair driver. Jill won and I came in second. The following year we competed in Cherbourg, then Saumur, in the Loire valley. I won the dressage on both occasions. The Cherbourg marathon was incredibly tough with very steep hills; I came second overall. At Saumur I won the dressage but made a silly mistake in one of the hazards which dropped me to second place overall, where I remained, despite a fast clear round in the cones.

The French driver, Jean-Claud, who was the winner, very graciously asked me to lead the parade into the arena where again I was inundated with prizes, including four magnums of champagne.

*The Dressage phase. Cherbourg FEI. Robin and Siggy
in their prime and in perfect step.*

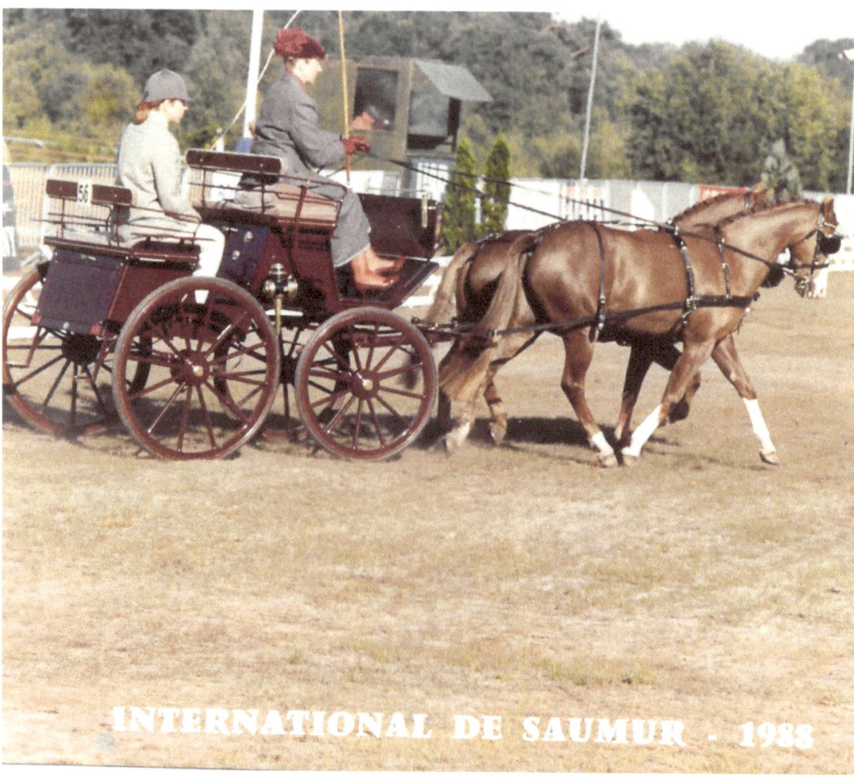
INTERNATIONAL DE SAUMUR - 1988

Compiegne near Paris

Relaxing in a stream, after the marathon Cherbourg

CHAPTER THIRTY-NINE

TAKING A BREAK

Several years after my accident, and the subsequent operations, on my hip, and the pain was dragging me down which made it difficult for me to compete. However, the ponies were fit and eager to go, and it is a whole lot easier to keep them fit while they are competing than to let them down for a year and then bring them back to fitness. The solution came to me unexpectedly! Loan my ponies to another pony pair driver for a season!

My respect and trust in John Pickford, a fellow pony pair driver, made my choice an easy one. Driving my cherished ponies, John Pickford became the points league champion.

The new pony that had joined us was Siggy. Siggy and Robin became soul mates, they were the perfect pair. Siggy was a pony that I had bought as a three-year old from a stud farm. The moment I saw her I knew I had to have her. She was the right colour and size to match Robin and had the sweetest temperament. I brought her on slowly and she worked so well with Robin and was such an asset to me.

John and Angie Pickford became close friends, and we would often go to stay with them at their home. We took the ponies with us for the weekend. When we went to Saumur, John and Angie came with us. Oh boy, did we have a lot of fun together!

During his driving career, John had not been very successful with his pair of ponies, despite being a very good driver. John heard of a pair of ponies that were for sale, but they were young and untrained. John decided to buy them and retired his other 2 ponies. He bought the ponies from Yogi, (Yogi was a very good driver in his own right. He was a professional, driving the Harrods coach around London). These new ponies were young sisters; Yogi broke them in for John. No problem there, except that they were inexperienced. John did not understand why he was not successful with them, I explained my theory/plan/forward programme to John. I had always used an experienced pony alongside a youngster. I had never driven two inexperienced ponies together before. It took me years of planning to achieve this ideal. Alpha taught Robin, Robin taught a succession of other ponies and gained huge experience. Then Robin taught Siggy.

One year after I bought Siggy I was given her full brother as a six-month-old foal, Coady, 'as a gift' I decided to keep him as a stallion to breed him with Alpha for two years running. That would be my new young pair of ponies for the future. This union produced Aladdin and Abby; just one year separated them When they were two years old, my groom, Julie, would stand on the back step of the carriage to lead them behind whenever we went out for short drives. By doing this they became used to traffic and the carriage wheels going round, and all the noises and sensations. As a result, they were fearless.

I recommended to John that he tried the same system with his pair. Alpha had gone out on loan to a farmer's daughter for retirement, leaving me with Siggy as my only mare. Because Siggy and Coady were full brother and sister we couldn't risk them getting together; the best option all round would be to sell Siggy to John. She would be his main lead pony. Believe me, selling my ponies was not something I did lightly, but Siggy had been with John for a year, she was comfortable in his hands, so I was happy for John to have her. Coady had already stepped into Siggy's driving shoes. He was bigger and stronger, so he took the pressure off Robin.

CHAPTER FORTY

CHINKS IN THE ARMOUR

I hadn't realized that Richard harboured resentment and that he felt that he was a dog's body while I got all the glory. There were a few times when Richard claimed that he could drive just as well as me, but he had never had the chance. We were out driving one day so this was an opportunity to let him drive home. Being well-known as a carriage driver had led me to becoming an instructor but Richard wouldn't let me tell him what to do.

We were driving on a tarmac road, and the ponies were going faster and faster. I noticed that Richard had little or no contact between himself and the ponies' mouths; the reins were slack. I asked him to slow them down a bit, but he snarled, "Just who's driving, me or you?" He used to say that I 'molly-coddled' the ponies, never pushing them to go faster. What was that all about? They went fast enough to win! Now, I told him that they were trotting too fast on a hard road surface. He threw the reins down and jumped out, yelling impetuously, "Do it yourself, I'm walking." Now, one of the golden rules of driving is that you never drive alone because you can't get safely to the horse's heads without losing control of them. Also, at road junctions when the ponies' noses are on the white line you are too far back to see what traffic is coming, Richard had put me in a dangerous situation.

On another occasion we went out in a single vehicle driving Coady, and Richard was driving along a country track. There were woods on the right and a barbed-wire fence on the left. About fifty yards up the track there was a large plastic bag that caught my eye; the bag was stuck on the barbed wire. Again, Richard had a very slack contact on the reins. Suddenly Coady spun round and in a nano-second we were heading home.

Richard shouted at me calling Coady "a stupid fucker," muttering, "What's wrong with him?"

"Well! didn't you see the plastic bag up there?"

"What plastic bag?"

I reiterated to Richard that; he would have felt Coady's anxiety if he had had better contact with the reins. Once again, Richard jumped out, throwing the reins at me. He walked home again. Turning Coady around, we went on for the drive, blowing away my frustration and a few cobwebs.

CHAPTER FORTY-ONE

REPAIRING THE CHINKS

We were feeling that we, as a couple, needed to get away so after selling Siggy to John and Angie we decided to treat ourselves to a holiday somewhere exotic. We went to Thailand, to Phuket Island to be exact. We stayed in Nai Yang at the Pearl Village, the only hotel on that beach in those days.

The beach mostly comprised of the peaceful Sirinat National Park, so I knew that it would be quiet. While we were there, we did a trial dive in the hotel swimming pool. I felt comfortable in and under water. When coming up for air, I told the instructor that I could hear a popping sound; he said that it was him putting air in my buoyancy jacket, and that there was no need to be worried. In the afternoon we went out in a dinghy into the bay to do a 'proper' dive. Everyone sat on the sides of the inflatable dingy, as did I, and then we all gently fell into the water backwards. The next thing I knew I was being hauled abruptly to the surface! I was asked why I had not put air in my buoyancy control device (BCD). I replied that no one had told me to!

When we returned home to England Richard decided that he wanted to take up scuba diving, so he joined a club. As a member of this club Richard made friends with one of the instructors. Together they decided to go into partnership and buy an ocean-going boat to do dive trips in the English Channel.

Richard spent increasing time on diving and less time with me and the horses. Detecting a rift between us, I secretly took myself off for scuba diving lessons. Once I got my PADI diver qualification, I proudly showed it to him, but his face fell a mile. He was not impressed that I was going to invade his new pastime. His comment was, "Just don't expect me to carry your oxygen cylinders for you."

I went out diving with him in the English Channel. Visibility was so poor that we descended to the anchor line. Richard told me to keep up with him, but I was struggling. He then went down deeper. I ended up swimming above him. He suddenly stopped and turned 360 degrees, obviously looking for me. Suddenly he went back at speed the way he had come. I turned to follow and got caught inside a large black cargo net. Keeping my wits about me, I backed out and started to surface. He was furious with me, ranting that I had ruined his dive, that he was not a babysitter! I never went diving with him again, but I kept up with my scuba activities. I preferred swimming in the sea with Robin.

This is the photo that Hew Graham sold for a lot of money.

Swimming in the sea with Robin off Selsey Bill

CHAPTER FORTY-TWO

THE DEMISE OF MY MARRIAGE

Richard and I had bought our council house under Maggie Thatcher's 'right to buy' scheme. We extended it and later sold it, buying a detached house a few miles away with the proceeds but pushing ourselves financially. However, that became a financial burden to us due to the housing market crash which affected all the UK.

Richard's business was also not doing so well, so I took on more shifts as a caregiver for people with learning difficulties. While I went to work on Christmas Day Richard spent the morning cooking a Christmas dinner; Lorna and Lou were on pony duties. Early afternoon, we were all expected to sit up at the dining table to eat a huge dinner! I could see Lorna and Lou's eyes pleading with me to do something. Instinctively knowing that they were overwhelmed by the piled high plates, my motherly advice was to eat what they could. Richard's fists came down on the table, as he shouted angrily, "I've been all morning doing this dinner!"

Richard used to constantly phone me at work to tell me he would be late home because he had to collect a car or get things done. So many 'reasons' why he had to stay out late. Finally, one night I'd arrived home after a late shift and Richard was sitting in bed, looking very upset. He said that we might lose the house.

My reply was not to worry, it didn't really matter to me. I'd lived in a caravan before and if we had each other we would be okay. Looking up at me with sadness he said, "You're not just my wife, you're my best friend and I love you." What he should have said was that 'he' might lose the house because he was having an affair with another woman and contemplating leaving! Three weeks later he came home from one of his diving trips and brazenly announced that he didn't love me anymore and that he loved someone else. As calmly as I could, and trying not to show my feelings, my response was,

"You had better leave then and take your stuff with you."

During that night, my heart broke into pieces.

The morning after I changed all the house locks. Lorna, still living at home, returned home to the aftermath. Lou, at that time, was living in Ireland. She was gutted by what Richard had done.

My heart was broken in more ways than one. Richard sited the ponies as the main reason he had left me, saying that he resented the time and money I spent on them (even though he revelled in the glory and social side that went with it). I knew that with or without him, they had to go! I gave some away, and I sold Aladin and Abby to a carriage driver. I sold the carriages and lorry and squirreled the money away.

THE END OF AN ERA!

PART TWO

CHAPTER ONE

ME, WHO AM I?

Not long ago, at a crossroad in my life, I had an identity crisis. I realized that all my life I've either been someone's daughter, someone's wife, or someone's mother!

> But who am I really? A lover of all things four legged, especially horses, dogs, and cats.
> Someone who has dared to dream.
> Someone who loves to travel due to a love of geography.
> Someone who has no regrets; life has made me who I am.
> Someone who has made mistakes but has learned from them.
> Someone who values friendships, a good listener and whose door is always open.
> Someone who does not like to be confined or controlled.
> Someone who likes to learn and share knowledge.

Someone who has strived to be the best daughter that I could possibly be.
Someone who is a good sister.
Most of all, the best mother, and grandmother I could ever be.

I am Me.

Galloping with the wind in my hair.
Or riding on a motorbike.
Maybe even flying high on the wind in a glider.

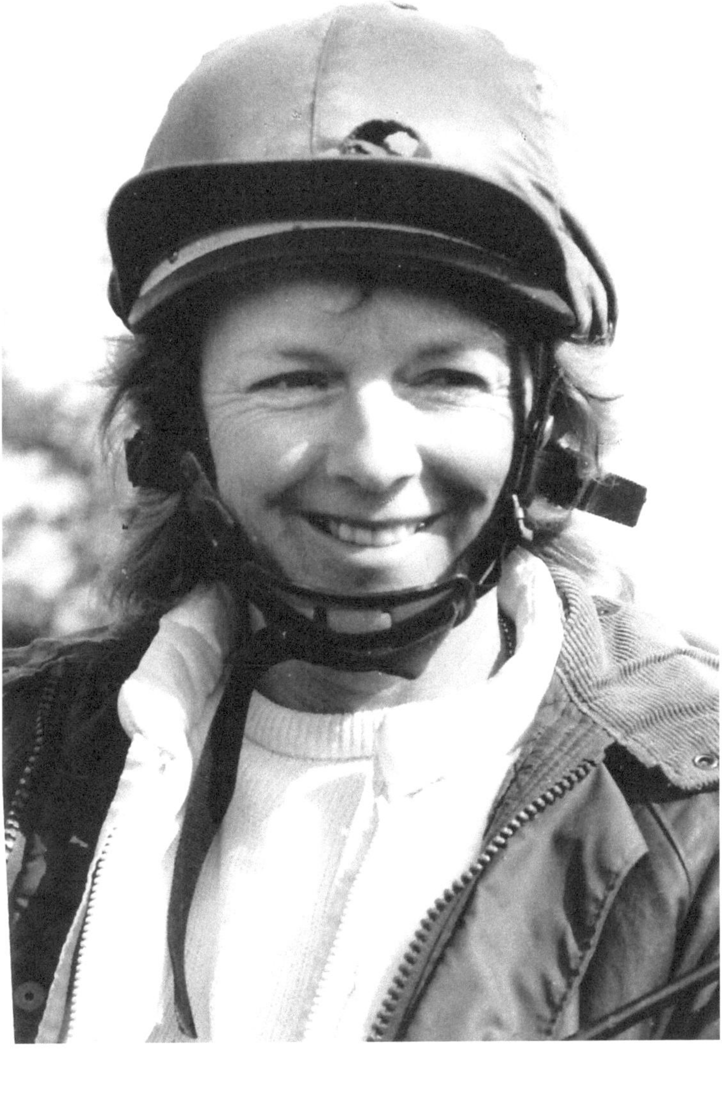

Honda CBR 650

A Glider lesson, yes, I took the controls.

Soaring high on the wind,
No sound but the whistle of the wind

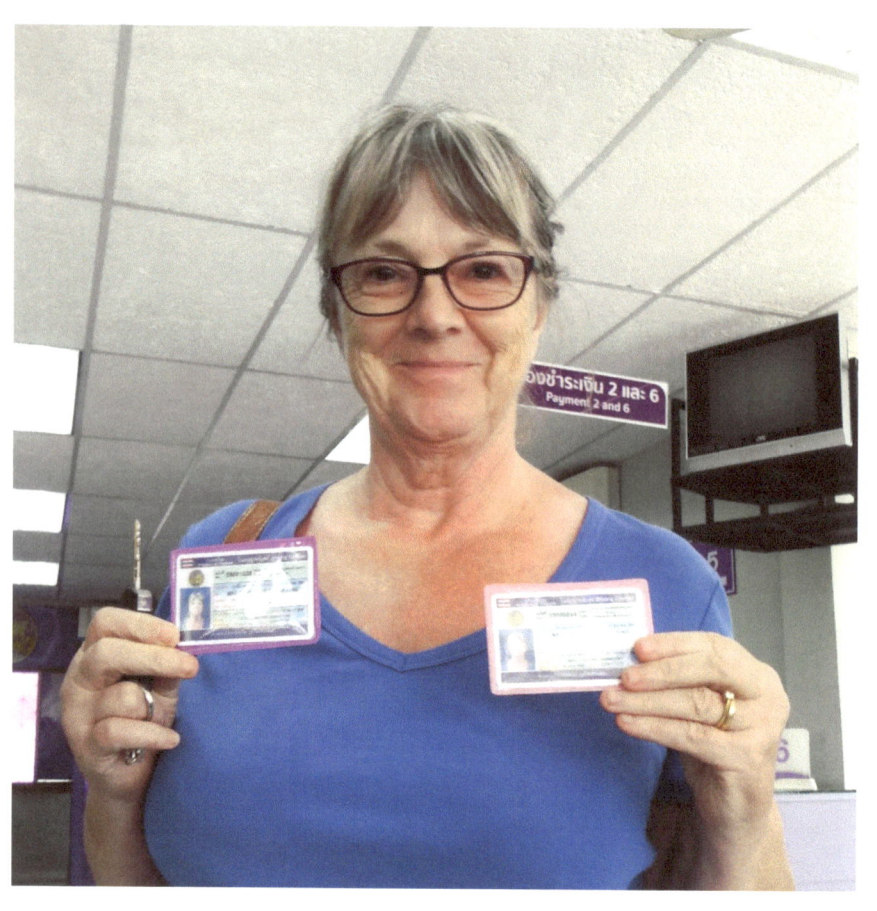

*Pleased as punch,
passed my Thai driving test for car and motorbike.*

Doing what I love. Socializing abandoned puppies at the dog pound.

CHAPTER TWO

MEETING GLEN

And moving to live in Thailand.

After living alone for 3 years, 1999 was the year that I met Glen. Every week, there was an over-30s disco club for singles. This was in a hotel on Bognor Regis Sea front. My friend, Diane, and I had been many times and had lots of friends. It was a Thursday evening club, and I got the opportunity to dance the jive with quite a lot of different men, which gave me the opportunity to let my hair down. One evening there was a new face there; it belonged to Glen. I was single. He was not.

In retrospect, my thought should have been that he should not have been there in the first place. He told me over a drink that he was working in the area for three weeks. I found him a tad exciting. Dating Glen at the time of my 50th birthday, helped me to overcome this milestone. He bought me a toilet seat as a present. No kidding! Bragged about it, too.

Glen finally went back to Leicester, but he tearfully phoned me and said that he didn't want to be there;

he wanted to be with me. But one thing remained to be done—he needed to sort his life out. Three months later he moved in with me. No money, no job, and no car! There is no fool like a middle-aged fool! Whenever I had a date, my lodgers insisted that they vet the man (more about my lodgers later). The funny thing was that they didn't like Glen much.

Two of Mum's sayings were, 'better to have tried and failed than never to have tried at all,' and 'better to have loved and lost, than never to have loved at all.' So, I embarked on a relationship.

Fortunately, all my lodgers had moved on by the time it became serious.

Since Lou's marriage had failed, Lou and her daughter, Fleur, had moved in with me, and now, so did Glen. The solution was to sell my 3-bed house to Lou and Lorna. Nick, Lou's ex-husband, gave me the money to buy a one-bedroom mews apartment for Glen and me to live in, all new furniture too. I used some of this money to pay for Glen and me to have a holiday in the far east, this included Nai Yang where I had been before with Richard.

When I lived alone, my two whippets, Tam and Bertie, a father, and son duo, slept on my bed, when Glen moved in, he didn't like it! So, they were banished. I came home from work one day to find them missing and on enquiring about them, was told that because we were moving into a flat where dogs were not allowed (untrue) Glen had found them a new home through the whippet rescue. I never found out where they were, but I did receive a photo of them basking in the sun on a window seat in a conservatory on a farm.

When Glen and I went to Nai Yang, he also fell in love with it. In 2001 Glen and I got married, on that day half of everything I owned became his.

That was certainly one decision that would give me regrets! Another decision that I would live to regret was to go to live in Thailand. Should we go? Or should we stay? That was the question. I remembered Mum's wise words, 'don't go and regret it—go, and if you regret, it at least you did it'. If I went, at least I would have tried. If it didn't work out, so be it. I don't want to go to my grave with regrets, nor with unfulfilled dreams and wishes! Having made the decision to go and give it a try we went! There were a lot of ifs and buts in those days.

In 2002, using some of the money left over from the sale of my house, we went in search of a piece of land to buy and build on. With the help of a Thai friend, we found the perfect spot. Then, in order to buy it, we had to see a Thai lawyer who informed us that we had to start a company that would buy the land (we as individuals) could not own land, but our company could. That company was Kingsacre Co Ltd. We still had a long way to go, moving money out there in stages to start the building work. We eventually moved out to live in 2008.

During the interim years, we went out to Thailand twice a year to check on things.

For a bit of fun and a surprise for Glen, I bought him a Honda 650 motor bike. We enjoyed it at weekends until one day Glen fell off it, so we sold it. Money just burns holes in my pockets. I just lavished him with gifs and surprises. I have frequently asked myself if I am a terribly slow learner.

Our honeymoon was spent in Jersey where I had been asked to give a talk about carriage driving, run a clinic and judge a competition; all expenses were paid. At our wedding breakfast, Glen got very drunk. Checking in for the flight to Jersey, the B.A. desk clerk diplomatically pointed out that I might have trouble getting him on the flight. However, we got there just the same. I spent the weekend doing talks, judging, and teaching while Glen played golf.

Glen joined a local gym and running club near where we lived in Westergate. He had his own agenda. He ran the London Marathon, no mean feat. He was out running straight after coming home from work. Near Christmas, the running club held their annual dinner and AGM in the pub 200 yards away from our apartment. When I asked, if I could go with him, he said, "No you can't, you're not a member and wives aren't included." Hang on a minute, there were husband and wife members. He said that was *different*.

I was, however, invited to a Christmas party that one of the running club members was holding. Keeping in mind that I didn't know any of his friends, this was quite daunting. The invitation card read, 'Champagne Buffet'. Just before we went, Glen went across the road and bought a six-pack of beer and a bottle of Lambrini light, alcohol-free wine, informing me that, as the driver I shouldn't drink. On arrival Glen gave the bottle to the host saying that it was for his wife as she was driving him home. This was way, way out of my comfort zone. Glen disappeared for one and a half hours during the evening. Arriving back, Glen told me that he had gone with the host to visit a neighbour, who had a problem with their boiler! Glen then spent the evening 'mixing and chatting,' surely the best euphemism for getting sloshed ever, while I propped up the sink. At 11pm, after telling Glen I would like to go home, we said our goodbyes, and thirty minutes later we finally left. On the way home Glen berated me and was verbally abusive about my demeanour, saying that he had to be drunk to tell me what he really thought of me.

The next day he brought me a cup of tea in bed, and I said, "Let's talk."

"What about," he said.

"Last night you wanted to talk to me. So now I want to talk to you." He couldn't remember a word of it and was sugary sweet!

In 2008 to fund our dream of retiring to Phuket we sold the apartment, the car, and cashed in my endowment policies, burning our bridges behind us, so to speak.

Many years later, to my dismay, I found out that Glen was leading a secret life! Promises that had been made were broken, dreams were dashed.

CHAPTER THREE

WHAT TO DO NEXT? THE MOVIES!

Living in Thailand has its bonuses. 'We' expats were sought after to be movie extras. In 2009 there were flyers being handed out in Nai Yang.

Wanted.
Movie Extras.

I contacted them, and a representative came to Kingsacre to fill in a form and take my photo.

It was one Saturday, about four weeks later, that I received a phone call asking me if I was available to go for a shoot the next day, which was a Sunday. Yes of course I was.

"OK, we'll pick you up at 4 pm.

Thinking, that was late to start filming, I asked,

"What time will we be back?"

"Next Friday," was the reply.

We drove to Khao Lak, where we met all the other ladies who were going to be in the movie. We were put up in a hotel and told to get some sleep and set our alarms for 3am as we were to be picked up at 4am!

No one knew what the movie was about. We all gelled as a team and felt very excited and were full of anticipation. The next morning, sure enough, at 4am a coach arrived to pick us up, and all bleary eyed, we were driven across to Phang Nha. It was a slow and winding route that seemed to take forever. We arrived at Phang Nha hospital, at 6am, where there was a magnificent buffet breakfast waiting for us.

After we'd eaten, we were all given a number to hang round our necks; I was number 36. On a board was a list of the numbers, and a description of which part we had been assigned. Number 36 was the mother of a young child! I felt flattered that, aged sixty, they thought the part of a mother of a nine-year old girl named Fabienne fitted me! One by one we went into the costume tent and were kitted out. From there we went into make-up. They asked, "Please can you take off your watch, hair band and glasses, when we start the filming?" The diligence by the make-up crew was incredible.

We had to be ready to go on set by 7.30am. When number 36 was called up on set. That was the moment I met my new daughter, a cheeky girl. Luckily for me

Fabienne fell asleep as soon as she lay down. I even had to wake her to go down for lunch. It was my task to explain to her that because she had been asleep, for 'continuity' she had to either go back to sleep or pretend to be asleep.

We all soon discovered that the movie was 'The Impossible,' staring Ewan MacGregor, Naomi Watts, and Tom Holland. We were told that under no circumstances should we tell anyone, nor approach the stars. And definitely we were not to take their photos. One woman did and was sent straight home.

On the third day a small group of us were asked to watch a video of the tsunami to enable us to get into our roles as survivors. That's when the penny dropped, the enormity of the subject of the movie—a true story of how a Spanish family survived the tsunami and were reunited. Naomi Watts played Maria, the mother of three boys. The original 'Maria' was on set with Naomi to talk her through her feelings during the actual disaster. The attention to detail was amazing.

I already knew that there was going to be a scene where a child dies. We were called up on set, and very soon realized that this was going to be *the* scene. Having watched the footage of the tsunami everyone was in sombre mood, and it was eerily quiet. There was some very sad music playing and a Thai nurse was singing a lullaby to a little girl. Looking at the now sleeping

Fabienne, I tried to imagine her to be my granddaughter, I was asked if I needed tear drops in my eyes that was definitely not necessary.

Take 1
Holding the sound asleep Fabienne's hands in mine against my face, which was wet with tears, our hands slid down into a position of prayer. The director was very excited by this and the natural way it had happened. He asked if I could repeat it and moved the camera up closer; this was going to be *the* take. Wow! It was very moving and intense, and from then on, I was no longer number 36, but Christine! It upset me a great deal, putting everything into perspective with regards to the tsunami, In the end, this scene was cut from the movie, and I can't say that I'm sorry.

Participating in a night shoot, and seeing Ewen MacGregor for the first time, was a particularly surreal experience. He was with the two young boys who played his sons, and the scene was when Naomi was taken to surgery. I participated in quite a few scenes with Naomi Watts and Tom Holland. Once, breaking protocol, I told Tom Holland what a fantastic piece of acting I had witnessed! He thanked me.

As a result of this movie, more movie work was offered to me, one being a German tsunami film which must have been done on a budget because I had to wear my own clothes, and they sent me to the back of a juggernaut lorry, which doubled up as the make-up lorry. I was told to sit in a black bathtub full of dirty water and swish it all over myself! (I did as I was told!) The day was spent running and screaming in soggy dirty clothes, a bit of a let down from what I had come to expect!

I did another movie down on Laguna beach, but I had no idea what it was about. Following on from this, two photo shoots for an English guy were in store for me. One was here on Phuket where; it was necessary to change into lots of different outfits. One minute I was a doctor, then a teacher, a nurse, and a boardroom executive with a pretend computer. When I enquired what they were all for the photographer said that he sold the photos all around the world to advertising companies to put up on hoardings for recruitment companies.

Number 36, with my on-screen daughter.

Night shoot

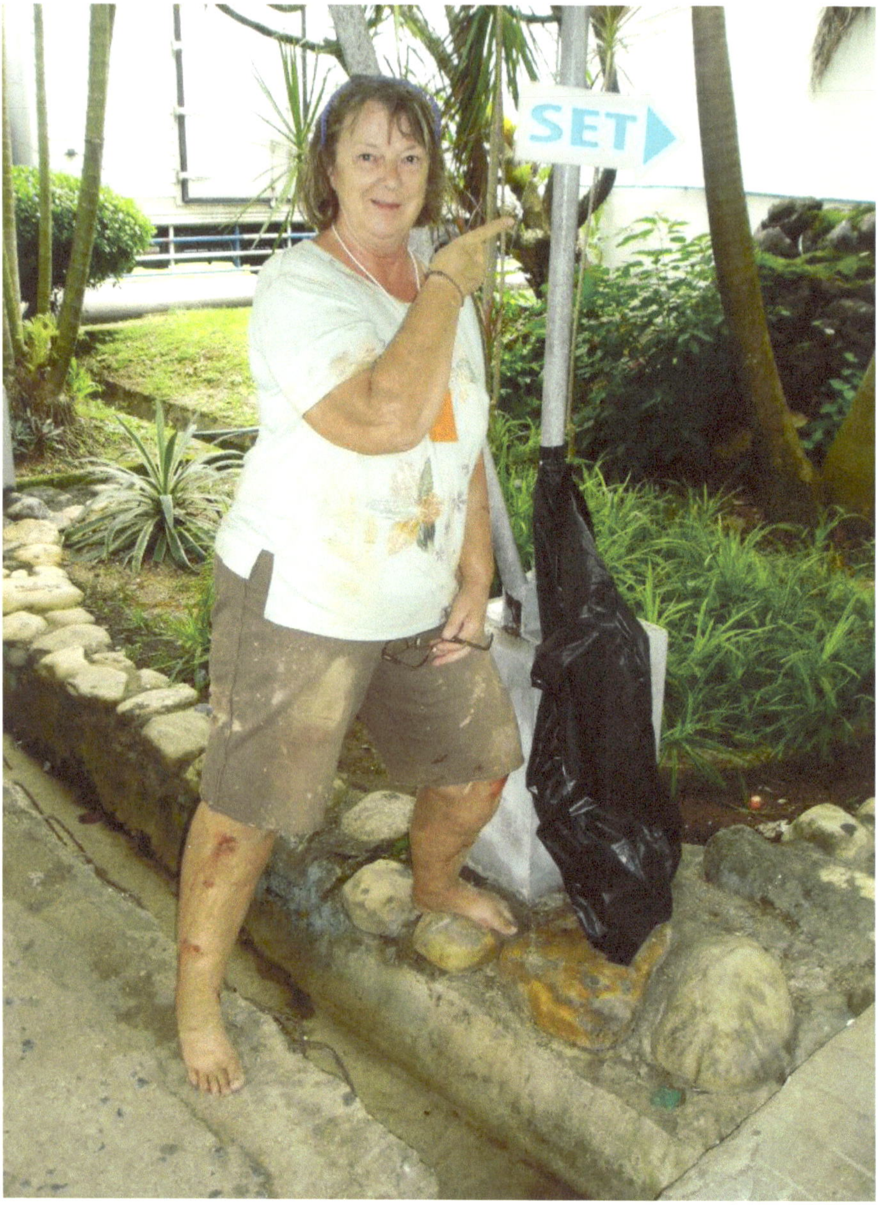
SET

CHAPTER FOUR

I AM NOW A FAMOUS DOCTOR.

Three years later

A friend emailed me a photo that she took when she was in Lithuania on holiday.

It was me as a doctor on a huge roadside hording. all written in Russian.

The second shoot that I did was, in Bangkok. All expenses were paid, and staying in a hotel enabled me to walk around the corner to the photo shoot. It was about schools and education, and this time I was supposed to be a teacher. These days were very long, although I was looked after very well. There were lots to eat and drink, but it was very tiring. This shoot paid well, and when I arrived back home in Phuket, I treated myself to a five-day detox. This is when I decided to become a vegetarian.

CHAPTER FIVE

My family, 1921–2021, A Full Century of Social History

Born in 1921, my father was an only child. He was sometimes a distant figure in my childhood. Dad grew up in Luton and from a young age he was fond of building balsawood airplanes and gliders. I don't know much about his childhood. The cold hard truth is that I hardly knew him at all.

James Victor Ginn

I remember my grandfather with great fondness. After walking home from school to save the bus fare, I would stop off at Grandad and Grandma Ginn's house. Grandad would be standing at the gate looking out for me, and he would give me an apple.

As a youngster Granddad was put into a children's home at a very early age because his parents were unable to take care of him. Now, he was not a well man; he had diabetes and thyroid problems that were never diagnosed, which meant he was very large around the middle. I was told that in World War 1 Grandad was a conscientious objector, and therefore he became a stretcher bearer for the duration.

Grandma Ginn, on the other hand, was a tiny woman. She had also been placed in a children's home as a child. It was probably how they met. God bless them both, their way of life had been dominated by their childhood, the war, rationing and hardship. Always appearing to be grubby in appearance, Grandma was also a hoarder, collecting and keeping anything and everything. You could hardly get into the house for stacks of newspapers from floor to ceiling. Grandma always wore a grubby coat and a beret, ankle socks and lace up shoes.

Grandma was a keen gardener and grew all her own vegetables; if she found an 'un-claimed' piece of land she would cultivate it. Grandma used the black soot from the fire grate to enrich the soil (perhaps that gave her the grubby appearance?). She was a well-known figure wandering around Luton town, frequently going through dustbins to salvage things. As a child I found this very embarrassing After Grandad died, Grandma became a frequent Sunday lunchtime guest, bringing home-grown vegetables with her.

After Lorna's birth, Grandma came to visit. When I put Lorna on her lap, her 2-week-old great granddaughter, she looked up at me with tears in her eyes. She later told me in private that no-one had ever let her hold a baby before. **Later,** Grandma would sometimes babysit for me in return for a home cooked dinner.

Grandma on Luton High Street.
This photo was in The Luton News.

Granddad at Mum and Dad's Wedding.

Dad wanted to join the RAF as a pilot but didn't pass the medical because he wore glasses, so he became a physical training officer (PTI) for the RAF instead. After the war ended, Dad was not allowed to go home; instead, he was sent straight to Germany to an air force base there. Dad's duty was to take care of thirty Germans who were being held in a cowshed. They were filthy and extremely sick with scabies. Dad swapped his cigarette ration with an officer to access the treatment for the scabies which he then shared out amongst them.

Kurt Ernst, his wife, Marianna, their two daughters, Angelica and Derta were among the thirty being held there. The girls were very young and very sick. Every time Dad went to the canteen for meals, he joined the queue with a very large tray with six plates on it; then took the extra meals outside and fed the Germans who were working on the air force base.

Dad was eventually put in prison for *'fraternizing with the enemy and stealing from medical supplies'*. Mum said that if Granny ever found out about that prison spell, she would never be able to understand what had happened. Eventually it came out that Dad had spent time inside. Mum told Granny that he had stolen an airplane! Our cousin Tony had overheard all about this and had disclosed the information to us. In his frustration Dad took an aircraft and buzzed the tower at Luton Airport, just before he was demobbed.

Dad helped the Ernst family and others who were living in the cowshed; the British had pushed them out of their homes. The RAF had taken over the aerodrome, and in one hanger they found a stash of gliders but were not sure if they were in good nick or not. One RAF officer enquired if there was a willing volunteer to try out a glider or two. Dad stepped forward. Having found out that Herr Ernst was a glider pilot, together they worked to get one airborne, which they did successfully. This cemented their friendship. Indeed, in a moment of intimacy, Kurt Ernst confessed to Dad that he never wanted to be in the war, all he wanted to do was go home to his wife and daughters. Dad admitted the same. Neither of them wanted to be at war.

Dad was still in Germany when we all moved to Luton. We hadn't seen him for a long time. Eventually he came out of the air force and rejoined us, but by then he was all but a stranger to us children. Once having been 'naughty' Dad wanted to spank me for it, and I remember telling him, that, "Only my Mum can spank me, not you." This air of cheekiness may have led to my future spate of spankings that my sister later told me about.

Once, I remember using the cooker gas gun to shoot down a wasp in the kitchen. Not content with just shooting it down, I 'cooked' it on the wooden windowsill. That evening when Dad had finished working in the shed, he burst into our bedroom. I was lying face down on the bed reading a book. He wasted no time and spanked me good and proper! Next morning, when I got up and went down for breakfast and school, Dad frog-marched me into the kitchen, and showed me the burnt windowsill, which was first time I knew why I had been spanked!

There is no beating about the bush: Dad was a very clever man. A draftsman by trade, he worked for Hawker Sidley at Luton airport. At Christmas, all the employees' children went into one of the hangars to get a present from Father Christmas. The queue was very long. When we got to the front, we were given an orange by a man dressed up in red! Big deal.

In his leisure time, Dad, being keen on gliding, helped at the London Gliding Club at the weekends Whenever a pilot flew cross- country the wind currents often took the glider in any direction. Therefore, a pursuit vehicle would follow it to bring the pilot and glider back home. This is what Dad used to do. If the glider crash-landed, as it sometimes did, Dad would also collect it and repair it back up to the *certificate of airworthiness* or C of A.

He may have been intelligent, but he also used to do some pretty silly things. Dad had a workshop at the Gliding Club. Whenever he was working on a damaged glider, he would drop a large plastic sheet down to prevent dust from billowing about. One day Stephen found Dad unconscious underneath it. Dad refused to wear a protective mask and had been overcome by the fumes. Stephen dragged Dad out, and most likely saved his life by doing so.

Speaking of some of the stupid things that Dad did, one day he was driving the Land Rover up a very steep hill in Luton in a very slow-moving column of cars. Dad said, "I'm fed up with this." He mounted the pavement and undertook the lot. On another occasion, when driving through the countryside at night, Dad stubbornly, never turned the car headlights on, probably due to habits developed during blackouts in the war. We were inevitably pulled over by the police. My sister told me that the policeman said to Dad, "I've met some idiots in my time, but you beat the lot." He never followed a map, using the sun and the stars to plot his journey, and if he went the wrong way, he would never turn around. He would rather shout at Mum for not telling him sooner that we had missed a turning. When he was alone, Dad went everywhere on his motorbike.

-1959

One weekend at the gliding club, Dad unexpectedly, took me up in a glider. We went up on a tow winch that my dad had to release when we had reached a good height. That gave a slight thump and a knocking sound as we were released. We flew up in a thermal over the top of

Dunstable Downs, and I distinctly remember the landing was very smooth considering it was onto grass. The flight was twenty minutes long.

Dad designed and built a sidecar by using the nose cone of a crashed glider for the front. Stephen had pride of place sitting in the front because he was tall, Barbara and I sat at the back (facing backwards). It was built with cubby holes for packing such things as a tent and our clothes. In 1954 we all went to Germany on this dad-designed three-wheeler cone vehicle for a holiday to meet up with the Ernst family.

We motored down to Dover and set up our tent on the top of a hill. I remember that night with a little fear, as a terrible rainstorm blew up. Dad gently let the tent down on top of us and told us all to hang onto it throughout the night. We surfaced in the morning to find that everyone else's tents had blown away and that some people were sleeping in the toilet block. That day we sailed over to Germany on the roughest crossing of the year. For me, it was thrilling; the ship was buffeted about, rocking from side to side, and going up and down.

Driving through the Black Forest, Dad pulled into a gateway, and we all got out of the sidecar, climbed over a gate, and pitched our tent on a track. In the morning, the sun glowed through the canvas tent giving a golden hue which woke me up, only to find that everyone had gone out. Looking out through the fly sheet I saw some deer on the track. Packing up the tent we set off to Bavaria, to the town of Oberammergau, where the Passion Play, depicting the crucifixion of Jesus, was held every ten years. At the age of six years, it all made a big impression on me. From there we drove to Kurt Ernst's house. Dad had a special friendship with Kurt Ernst, Mariana, Angelica and Derta. We stayed with them for 5 days, and I fell in love with a blonde boy wearing 'lederhosen'.

Here are some extraordinary things that Dad did while serving in the RAF. He saw a plane flying low and knew it was going to crash. It crashed into the toilets Dad had just come out of, then burst into flames. The officer in charge asked Dad why he had not gone to rescue the people inside. Dad explained that the flames were underneath, where the men should get out of the plane and, sadly, he could not save them. Another time, whilst on a training exercise throwing live hand grenades for practice a 16-year-old cadet had a grenade in his hand and was frozen with fear and couldn't move. The officer in charge told Dad to get the grenade off the boy. Dad said the boy stood shivering and shaking, and he had to prize the lad's fingers off the grenade and then throw it.

Dad was undoubtedly a clever man, but not a good father in my eyes. He left the family home when I was thirteen. He had been having an affair with his secretary, Marie. One day, after Dad had left and Ted, Mum's new boyfriend, had moved in, Barbara, Stephen and I were washing the dishes; Barbara washed, Stephen dried, and I put away. Being the little minx that I was, I was kicking Stephen in the shin and saying, "Now Dad isn't here, you're the man of the house, so go ahead, kick Ted out!" Ha! That was like asking for the moon.

Barbara must have told Dad about my plan to leave home and live in a bedsit in town. Dad came over to ask me why? At that moment in time, finding it very difficult to express myself, I kept my thoughts and feeling inside me; it was impossible to find the words to tell him how I felt. Dad drove me and my belongings over to my new bedsit. A few years later, finding myself pregnant at seventeen, my wedding was a 'fait accompli' and I asked Dad to come to the ceremony and give me away, which he did.

When Lorna was six weeks old Dad emigrated to live in South Africa with Marie and her three children. Dad later left South Africa and moved to Rhodesia where he worked in a Diamond Mine office. He continued with his passion for flying. He was commissioned to design and build a private single seater small aircraft from the drawing board to flying it. He jumped at the chance to do this and arranged for an old test pilot friend to come over to take it for its inaugural flight. Happily, it turned out a success. Dad was under the impression that it would go into production, to sell to landowners who lived in the middle of nowhere, but this was not to be! It was sold as a one-off to a private buyer. No doubt Dad felt let down and disappointed! His marriage to Marie did not last, and Dad moved to Botswana. He used to write to me once a year telling me all sorts of stuff about an African woman he had met named Flora. After that he had a succession of African wives: Flora, Gladys, Bonny and then Hilda.

Eventually, Dad came over to the UK for a holiday. He stayed a week with me at Pitlands farm and he gave me a gift, some Zulu beads that he had bought in a market. Dad showed me a photo of Flora; she was 'traditionally built,' as they euphemistically term larger ladies in Africa. He asked me to take him into Chichester where he bought lots of colourful underwear, petticoats and panties for Flora, all size 10!

Two years later Dad invited Stephen and his wife, Marylyn, and their two young sons to visit him. Dad took them sight-seeing to Victoria Falls.

Unexpectedly, Dad sent me a photo of a small boy, saying, that he was his son, Daniel. Shortly after that dad asked me if I could come over to Africa. Naturally, I thought that this was my turn for a holiday, but Dad had other plans. He wanted me to help him get his son out of the country, explaining that a single man would have a lot of obstacles to overcome, but, if he were accompanied by a woman, it would be easier. I asked Dad if Flora knew about his plan to take Danny out of the country. It turned out that Gladys was Danny's mum, not Flora. Traditionally in Africa, a child born outside of marriage was the property of the mother's father. This man wanted to sell Danny to Dad; instead, Dad married Gladys, registered Danny as his son, then divorced her! Danny was about two years old then, while Dad was in his early seventies. I wrote back telling Dad directly that this was not going to happen Under no circumstances was Dad going to live with me, nor could he expect me to take care of Danny.

That gave me the opportunity to give Dad a piece of my mind. I asked him, "Where were you when, as a single mother I needed help?" Some months later, in November, when I was living at Woodend on a shoestring, an envelope arrived, no explanation in it—just a 10 rand note. Changing it at the bank, I found it was worth about £5. A few days later another one arrived with a 20 rand note in it, again no letter. This continued for some weeks leading up to December. I was feeling grateful. It was easy for me to spend it all on new clothes for my girls and second-hand bikes. The last but one envelope had 60 rand in it. I was eventually asked at the bank if I had been to Africa because, on this occasion, exchanging too much money had raised suspicions. Of course I had been there with my daughters (a bold-faced fib). As there were three of us, they gave me permission to exchange it. From that, I learned a valuable lesson—when the next envelope's load of money arrived, the wise choice was to take it to several different banks. There was never a covering letter with any of the money. After Christmas the elusive letter arrived from my father. Oh, my word! True to form, it said that he hoped that all the money had been put into a post office account for him for when he came to England! It's not difficult to imagine what my reply was. I told him that I had spent it all. It was some time before he contacted me again.

When Danny was six years old, Dad said that he wanted to bring him to the UK. I was constantly telling Dad directly that if he did, Danny would most probably be taken into care because, with Dad being in his seventies, it would be deemed to be an unsuitable situation.

One day while I was at work, Mum phoned me and told me in a querulous voice that, since her day had been ruined, she was now going to ruin mine. She then informed me that Dad had called her from Gatwick where he was with Danny and wanted MY address. The cheek of it!

At eight o'clock that evening Stephen phoned; Dad was in Weymouth with Danny. He had intended to go by ferry to Guernsey where a lady whom he had been chatting with on Dateline lived, but she had told him where to go in no uncertain terms!

Stephen rang him back with instructions from me, to get back to Chichester where it was possible, that, having connections in Social Services I might be able to help him. What do you know? The next day Dad called. Chichester Council had put him in a ground floor flat at the back of the Tesco Shopping Mall. He was thrilled. What! I definitely wasn't.

Out of curiosity, I made a rather spontaneous decision. I drove over to see him and my new young half-brother. My shock and immediate realization was that Danny was semi-wild! Probably he'd never had to toe the line in his life. He'd not learned to speak English, a fundamental requirement in life here. Danny spoke pidgin English, mostly *gimmee, gimmee*. He poked his little hands into my pockets and bag, ran around turning lights on and off, and was wearing nothing but a pair of Y front underwear. He had clearly never seen electric lights before. Dad confirmed this when he showed me a photo of the shack where they lived—dirt floor and mattresses.

Danny got the vacuum cleaner out and ran amok with it. Then in his own language Danny asked Dad for money—*gimme, gimme.* When Dad refused Danny opened the front door, picked up the TV (a relatively small one) and was about to throw it out. Dad stopped him by giving him his purse. Danny flung some clothes on and went over to Tesco. Some time went by before Dad had a phone call from a representative of the store who said that Danny was at the checkout with a load of sweets but not enough money. Dad told them to give him what he could afford and send him home.

Six months later, Dad and Danny were moved to a flat just outside Bognor Regis. I tried to help Dad by providing him with some essentials and the occasional stew and visited him every week. Perhaps at last an opportunity had arisen for us to get to know each other? Danny was eventually taken into care, because he was found at 10 o'clock at night with some older boys on Littlehampton train station.

I bumped into Dad one morning in Tesco. He invited me to join him for a coffee. Guess who paid? Dad then dropped the bomb shell—he was going back to Botswana. 'They' had taken away from him the only thing he cared about—Danny! That felt just like a cold wet flannel had smacked me in the face. What about his other three children?

I followed Danny's progress through school. I felt slightly akin to him, as he'd joined the ranks of the children that Dad had left behind. Danny had no idea who I was. He called me 'mum'. He was eventually sent to a residential school for boys, and I found out that he was doing very well and was well liked by the other boys. His teacher said that he could become a lawyer or a doctor. Soon Danny went to mainstream school in Chichester, and I met up with him when he was sixteen. By then he knew that I was his sister, but he found it hard to become reconciled to the fact.

Eventually, Dad bought Danny a one-way ticket back to Africa when he was 16 ½, under the pretext that the lad was going to visit Gladys. The truth was that dad wanted Danny to work and eventually manage dad's sweat-shop clothes factory.

Before Dad went back to Botswana, he gave me his pension book (this was to ensure that on the 5th April his pension would go up!) asking me to cash in the next three weeks' money and put it in his bank. Dad also told me not to let 'them' know that he was gone. I am sure that this was highly irregular and illegal. I was naïve, too.

Barbara came down to help me clear out his messy, filthy flat. She took some things home; other stuff came home with me. A week after he left, a letter arrived from Dad saying that he was in Gaborone, and it was monsoon season. Another week on, and another letter arrived saying that this might be his last letter (to me, clearly a mock-suicide letter). Another week went by, and his next letter explained that he had met 'the woman of his dreams'. Her name was Bonny, and he was on his way to meet her parents.

Dad had written asking me to send him some passport photos that were in a suitcase that he had left behind. Being so angry, I posted the whole lot to him—photos, keys to the flat, plus his pension book—to his address in Botswana. I sent it all off on a Saturday. The following

Monday there was a knock on my door. Lo and behold, who was there waving his arms about saying that he wanted the keys to his flat? Dad! I was beside myself exclaiming that they were on their way to Botswana. Then I took a deep breath, and said, "Hang on a moment, I do have things that belong to you, and I fetched all his bills and red letters. Shoving them all in his hand, I told him to go away and not to come back.

Dad's marriage to Bonnie only lasted a year. Then Dad was back in the UK in a confusing sequence of events, for me anyway. When I saw him around Bognor, I looked the other way. After toing and froing to Botswana and back, Dad had divorced Bonny. Then he married Hilda and brought her to the UK. How does he manage it? 'They' offered him yet another council house. Dad constantly, moaned about the UK; he didn't like the cold, wet winters. But flying backwards and forwards whenever the mood took him, he said he didn't like the hot dry summers in Africa, either.

Where did the money come from? One Christmas day, Dad arrived at East Midlands airport declaring himself homeless. He was put up by the airport for the night, then given the train fare to Nottingham where my sister lived. Dad was subsequently given a flat in sheltered housing. By now he was in his 80s.

Hilda claimed to be Dad's carer and travelled back and forth from Botswana to the UK every year. I have no idea where the money came from. This saga went on year after year.

A few years later, meeting up with Stephen at Barbara's house, Stephen impulsively suggested that 'we' really 'ought' to pay Dad a visit. Barbara knew where he lived so we all went round there. I made it clear right from the word go that I wasn't going to go in. Barbara and Stephen tried hard to persuade me. I sat outside in Barbara's car reading a book, adamant that I would not go in. Then Barbara came out again, |I felt under such enormous pressure that I ended up 'giving in'. I had so much hatred and anger inside me, and I was very unsure what might happen.

I went in hand in hand with Barbara and met Hilda in the hallway; she seemed like a genuinely decent person. And there was Dad, sitting in an armchair. He got up, and tried to hug me, but I recoiled. Stepping back, I said, "You know you really hurt me." Dad waved it aside, saying, "Oh, that! That's all in the past..." Not for me it wasn't. I desperately wanted him to say sorry, but he couldn't. This could have turned the clock back.

Dad passed away on 10th August 2017. My half-brother Danny asked me to send him £10 to help pay for a flight over to come to the funeral. Danny wanted to bring his wife and two children to the UK, (he explained that he would get a house and benefits if he could get over here). As far as I am aware Danny is still managing

Dad and Hilda's clothes sweat-shop factory using the old treadle Singer sewing machines and hand sewing machines that Dad had sourced while on holiday in the UK.

Stephen offered to help Hilda with the funeral expenses. Except for Barbara and Stephen, the entire congregation was black. Some people flew over to England from Botswana to attend. Stephen got the invoice for the funeral from Hilda, complete with entries for a new dress and coat, a new hat, shoes, handbag, stockings, and necklace. Dad taught her well. Sorry, sarcasm doesn't become me! Danny has my email address and Facebook name; sadly, he only contacts me when he wants money.

Stephen posted this Obituary in a Gliding magazine.

Obituary James Victor Ginn
1921 to 2017

It is with sadness that I write to inform you of the death of my Father, James Victor Ginn, (better known to friends and colleagues as 'Vic Ginn'). These are my recollections of his life – I apologize if there are any inaccuracies.

He was born in Luton in 1921. His parents came from London. He was educated in Luton and served an apprenticeship on wooden aircraft at the Percival

Aircraft Company at Luton airport. He married and joined the RAF towards the end of the war. He was posted to Germany at the end of the war to Lubeck, near Hamburg, where he was taught to fly gliders by an officer of the German Air force using a Dagling/ Zogling basic trainer. The officer's name was Kurt Ernst.

On his return to the UK, he moved to Eastbourne and joined the South down Gliding Club at Friston near Eastbourne. His logbook records my first flight in a T21 at the age of 4½. He recorded that he was P2! Draw your own conclusions! He told me of a flight he did in a Scud where for a while he unintentionally dropped below the clifftop while soaring but managed to avoid landing on the beach!

In 1950 we moved to Luton when he managed to get a job at Hunting Percival Aircraft Company as a draughtsman. Some of his work was on the Jet Provost aircraft. He joined the London Gliding Club and in 1953 he began designing and building the Kestrel glider. He had involvements there with the Scud, Gull, and Slingsby Sky gliders. From then on, he spent much of his spare time maintaining and repairing gliders. Some of the repairs were drastic: broken wings and fuselages. At one time he bought an Olympia, which was an insurance write off, rebuilt it back to an airworthy condition and sold it on. He replaced the cockpit area using a ply/balsa sandwich as used on the Mosquito aircraft.

By 1966, when he emigrated to South Africa, he had become Inspector, then Senior Inspector of the BGA. Shortly after arriving in South Africa, he moved to Rhodesia and joined a gliding club there where he did another extensive repair. He also worked for the railways and, during UDI, worked maintaining Canberra reconnaissance aircraft. He later moved to Botswana where he worked in the DeBeers diamond mines as a draughtsman.

My father returned to the UK infrequently until a few years ago when he had a heart pacemaker fitted but was generally in good health and remained quite active, even doing small DIY jobs, until early this year.

He passed away on 10th August 2017 after a short illness.

Stephen Ginn

I was living in Thailand at this time, **and** not able to attend his funeral, but I remember his passing with sorrow, for what could have been.

Dad all smiles at the Clubhouse, in the glider, surrounded by club members.

*Stephen outside our house with a glider trailer.
Dad was very shrewd; he inserted one window in the van,
keeping it registered as a van, not a dormobile!*

Working on his glider in the huge shed which is now housed in a museum in Wattisham, Lincolnshire.

Our iconic motor bike and side car. Dad built it from the nose cone of a crashed glider. As children we loved it. Here we are posing in it outside Granny's house, in Eastbourne.

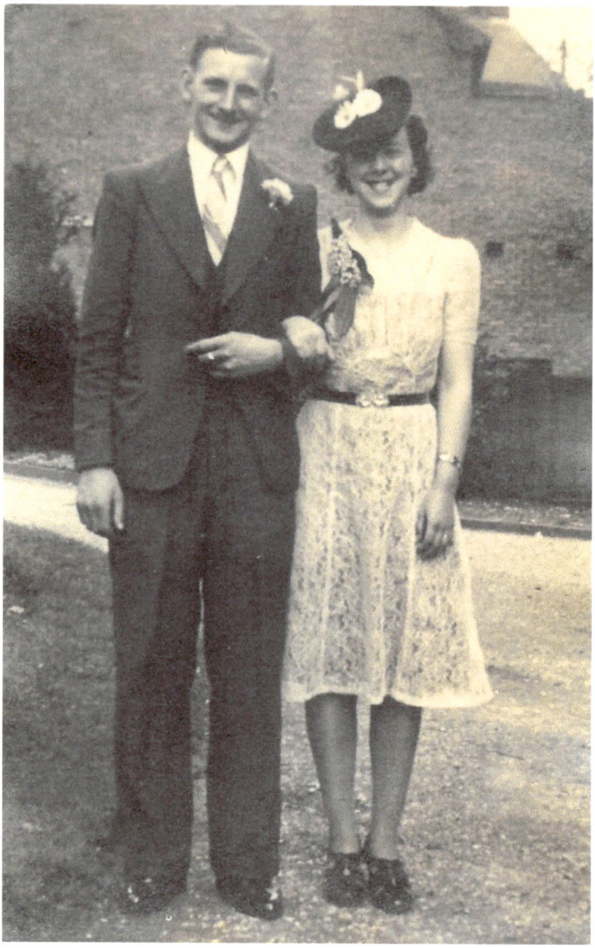

CHAPTER SIX

My Mum

If I was asked to describe my mum this is what I would say. She was 5ft 2in with dark hair, a kind face, hard-working, and seemed to be able to do a hundred things at once; she was very supportive of her entire family, and never judged. A very fit and healthy lady: she loved to travel, was good at telling stories and loved to chat, speaking with a voice that carried. She called a spade a spade, didn't suffer fools gladly and said what she meant. She was not appreciated by Dad for all she did, and I didn't truly appreciate her until I became a mother myself.

Mum was born in Eastbourne on June 15th, 1923, and christened Lillian May Chatfield. She was one of four children: her eldest brother was Fred, then came a sister, Dorothy, Mum was number three, and last, but by no means least, came little brother, Ronald. Uncle Ron was a sickly child who suffered badly with eczema, the treatment for this was quite brutal at that time and it took Grannie's attention away from her other children.

Mum grew up in Eastbourne. She told me how they all went out on Sundays in a pony and trap. The roads were narrow lanes with the countryside not far away. Mum's favourite flower is the gardenia; she remembers the porter at the hotel where she worked collected gardenias to decorate the breakfast table, and the perfume floated in the air for ages.

From an early age Mum loved to travel, even if it was just around the south of England. She didn't know what travel adventures were in her store for her in her future. She was evacuated to Cirencester during the war because the south coast was a very dangerous place, as it was constantly being bombed. There was also a fear that any invasion could come in through there.

One place that we frequently went to as a family in the Land Rover was Brancaster on the Norfolk coast, where we camped. Mum didn't really enjoy these holidays: it wasn't really a holiday for her at all, because she had us three kids to look after and meals to prepare. Dad had a small dinghy, and spent most of his time in it, with Stephen as co-skipper. We had a beautiful border collie dog called Sue, but she was not a well dog, being prone to fits. Susie had a fit in the water as we were walking along the sand together. Mum rushed to her side and got her out very quickly. Most days, us girls searched for cockles and shrimps. We also found some edible sea grass that we gathered up, and Mum made us a delicious meal with fresh bread.

On one of these holidays, Mum said that she wanted to learn to drive. Dad drove the Land Rover down onto the vast, empty beach, and gave Mum a very short driving lesson. Off she went! We kids were hysterical with laughter and pretended to be scared, hanging our feet over the tail gate for a quick escape.

Once, as a family, we went to the Island of Jersey at the time of 'the festival of flowers, where people made carnival floats with flowers. At the end of the day the traditional Battle of the Flowers took place where everyone starts to rip the flowers off the floats and throw them at each other. We were camping in a farmer's field, and Barbara and I took turns to go down to buy Jersey milk from the farmer each morning. But most of our holidays were spent in Eastbourne: Easter, Christmas, and summer school holidays, sleeping on mattresses on the bedroom floor of Granny's house, the three of us and our cousin Tony.

One night Barbara and I were walking from Lower Road to Granny's. It was quite late and dark, and we saw a man walking along the road towards us, so we crossed over. Then *he* crossed over, too. We were getting scared, so we crossed back again. Then the man shouted at us to stop messing about! It was Uncle Fred, Mum's oldest brother, who had come to find us. Uncle Fred was my favourite uncle. He was an elusive man who spoke few words, and to me he appeared to be very tall. He wore a Navy uniform and looked very grand. Granny fussed over him, and at that time we didn't know what tragedies he had seen.

My New Stepfather

After Mum's marriage ended, she worked at the Electrolux factory for more money to take care of us. While Mum was working there, she met Ted, and he moved into our house and eventually bought Dad's share out for £700! Once Mum and Ted were married, they travelled together all over Europe, mostly on organized coach trips. I can't say that I liked Ted much, but it was Mum's choice and she seemed very happy. Luckily, they shared a desire to travel. There wasn't a country in Europe that they didn't visit. Mum and Ted were married for 30 years until he died, so you could say that I knew him longer than I knew my own father. We both mellowed over the years.

When Ted was ill in the Luton and Dunstable Hospital, Mum was very upset because he seemed to have the early stages of dementia and was being abusive, he thought Mum was having an affair with the doctor. From my own working experiences, knowing that dehydration could result in confusion, I encouraged Mum to get him to drink more, a difficult task. I drove straight up the M1 motorway to visit him and gave him a stiff but kind talking to. Ted was under the impression that Mum was back with Dad, and that was why he was 'put in hospital'. He had, in fact, fallen and broken his leg while on holiday with Mum in Great Yarmouth. He was in a pitiful state for a man who prided himself on being well presented, with a tidy haircut, and now here he was, crying. The nurse told me that he wouldn't let her take care of him, nor help with his oral health care. I offered to take over from her, and Ted was very compliant with me. I told him how much Mum loved him, how he had been a good father to me over the years, and a good grandfather to Lorna and Lou. He looked at me with tears in his eyes. 'Is that true? he said.

There were things about Ted that no one knew regarding his early life. He had been a prisoner of war and was terrified of any nurse that looked like they were Japanese. This included a Filipino nurse, or anyone from the Far East. When I arrived at Mum's house she burst into tears. I comforted her, telling her that I had already been to see Ted. That afternoon we both went to visit Ted, taking with me the means to wash and cut his hair and shave him. He was quite different then. Ted was later transferred to a care home within walking distance from

Mum's house. We went to see him; he was still a difficult man to take care of.

After Ted died, and a period of mourning had passed, Mum went travelling on her own—coach trips all over France and Germany, including a trip up the river Rhine. It was my pleasure to take Mum on a trip to the Isle of Lewis in the Outer Hebrides to visit Lou, Nick, and Fleur. Nick took us up in the 'search and rescue' helicopter, and Mum was thrilled and very proud. Mum regularly went to Majorca because two of her grandsons (Stephen's sons) live there, Jeremy and David. Mum even took Aunty Dorothy with her once. Aunty Dorothy was approaching 80 years of age at the time and had never had a passport before!

Another holiday that Mum and Aunty Dorothy went on was to Cornwall. There was a navy museum there, so they went in. They were looking at a cabinet of navy cap badges and Mum, whose oldest brother Fred served on the battleship HMS Ajax, said, studying them, "there isn't a cap badge for HMS Ajax." A man standing behind them explained that everything connected to HMS Ajax was in a museum in Canada.

I looked it all up for Mum on the internet, and sure enough, just south of Toronto was a town called AJAX. I contacted the town's offices, and a very helpful lady told me they were soon to be celebrating the fiftieth anniversary of the founding of the town. During the war people from all over USA and Canada were called to help with making munitions for the war, which were then sent across the north Atlantic in convoy. Thousands of people came forward and they lived and worked there together for the duration of the war. They made friends and formed relationships, married, and had families. When the war was over, they were told to go back home, but many felt that this was their home! The town of Ajax is just south of Toronto in Canada; it was created so that all the munition workers could make it their permanent home to live in. All the streets in Ajax are named after the crew who fought in the war on the ship, HMS Ajax. Sure enough, we were told that there was a road named Fred Chatfield Drive.

We were asked if we would like to attend the celebrations of the fiftieth anniversary. If we could do so, the town would arrange a tree planting ceremony for us in Chatfield Drive, attended by the Mayor of Ajax, all arrangements would be taken care of. There would be a gala banquet and celebrations, and a tree planting ceremony in Fred's memory. That was an easy decision!

Mum, me, Lorna, and Fleur, my granddaughter, all four generations attended. At the gala dinner, a very young-looking woman in Mounty uniform greeted us. Mum, with her usual curiosity and innocence asked,

"Are you a real Mounty?" she smiled and said, "Yes, I am a real Mounty."

This lady, was not an actress or a prop, she was a guest of honour. It was a night to remember for us, lots of speeches, **followed by dancing and then** early to bed because we had another big day to follow—the tree planting.

Me, Fleur, 'the real Mounty' Mum and Lorna at the gala dinner.

The tree planting.

The town mayor was there with us. Mum was overwhelmed and broke down. The mayor comforted her, and yes, that is the mayor in shorts. It was a very moving and fitting moment in time. There were several other guests who were also planting trees in honour of their relatives. We all supported each other.

To lift our spirits, while we were in Canada, we travelled on an amazing double decker train, and we took trips out which included a visit to Niagara Falls. Seeing is believing! It was staggeringly impressive, a truly memorable trip for us all. Of course, we had to sail on the 'Maid of the Mist' right into the bottom of the waterfall.

Then we went into a tunnel inside the water fall to a viewing station, it was extraordinary! To follow this, at Fleur's request, we had lunch in the iconic Niagara Falls Hard Rock Café: burgers of course!

We caught the train back into Toronto, and then there was a boat ride round Lake Ontario, which was followed by our next challenge, to go up to the top of the CNN tower, to walk on the glass floor and have lunch in the revolving restaurant. Lunch first because we were famished, and after lunch we went up to the glass floor. It was the most surreal experience. In hindsight we should have gone there before lunch! We couldn't walk on it!

We went there two days running to try and pluck up the courage to do it, but there was no way in this world any of us could stand on it. We felt an irrational fear; it was like looking down at the 'ants' on the walkway below. It was hysterically funny, and we all fell about laughing. In between the two glass floors was what must have been a steel girder. We tip-toed along it, so that we could stand with our backs to the wall for a photo! Along the back wall was a large mural of hippos with a sign saying that the glass floor could carry the weight of 9 hippopotami! My fertile imagination went wild, HOW DO THEY KNOW THIS? I was visualizing 10 hippos falling through the sky, all legs flying out with a broken glass floor above them! A funny and exciting time, with moments of sadness and glory; Mum had so many tales to tell on her return.

Mum carried on with her desire to visit new places and when she was 79 years old, she came with me on a three-week tour of China. On leaving Beijing, very early one morning on a train to Manchuria, no sooner had the train got going, than it turned into a marketplace. The train staff came up and down the train peddling their wares; it was amazing fun, not knowing what was coming next. In Manchuria we went to where the Dali Llama once lived. Stupid me! I paid a monk to release a bird, which promptly flew round and back into the cage for the next mug.

Fleur hanging onto Great Grandma On the edge of. the glass floor

*Lorna and Fleur almost on the glass floor,
well, laying on it at least. Do not look down!*

A coach then drove us back to Beijing to catch another flight to Wuhan, from where we sailed up the Yangzi River, passing through the three gorges where we saw the construction of the new Yangzi River Dam. Nothing can prepare you for the size and scale of it. Sailing further on, we had to face the reality that thousands of Chinese farmers would lose their homes once the dam was complete. On arrival in Chongqing, a cultural concert was arranged for us.

The next flight took us to Xian where the terracotta army is located, yet one more mind-blowing thing to see. Then it was back to Beijing. In my mind's eye I can still see Mum trying to do Tai Chi in the park with Chinese folks. Once, Mum was using a broom to mess about, trying to do Tai Chi, and a fellow traveller said very loudly, "You should ride that, you old witch," but it was all in fun. No offence was taken; Mum loved to be right in the thick of it. We walked the Great Wall and Mum bought a T shirt that said, 'I Walked the Wall".

Wherever we went Mum was like a magnet to the Chinese people who marvelled at her age. Once, she saw some Chinese people spinning the prayer wheels and asked about them; subsequently Mum walked along spinning the wheels and reciting the Lord's Prayer. A crowd gathered around her to listen to this prayer which she gladly explained. Then, of course, there was the obligatory photo call.

Mum was a keen church club attendee and often gave little talks. After she got home from China she went to the club and everyone wanted to hear all about her trip, Mum stood up wearing her jacket. She said, "For the first time in my life I can honestly say, been there, done that," and flinging her coat open she said, "and I got the T shirt." What a whirlwind trip that was, we were filled with awe and laughter in equal amounts.

Mum came to Thailand with me twice, staying with me in our newly built house that we would eventually live in once we retired. It was important to me that Mum could see where I was going to live. She commented to me one day that she would not like to live here in Phuket, and I asked her why. She said that she didn't like "that bog pointing down towards our land". I told her, "That's not a bog, Mum, that's the water meadow. I used to see a herd of water buffalo coming up through the garden every morning before they wandered off down into the village.

When Mum was in her 80s, she went with Barbara to Australia to visit Barbara's daughter, Larisa, who had emigrated there. Mum was away for 5 weeks. In hindsight, it took its toll on her. I arrived in the UK the day after mum got back from Australia, and it shocked me how thin and frail she felt when I hugged her. Mum later told me that she had been waiting for 'someone' to tell her not to go. Knowing Mum as I do, she would not have liked to be told what she should or shouldn't do, and she'd have ended up blaming that 'someone' for her not going.

Very soon I realised that Mum couldn't cope living on her own in her house. She admitted that she needed to have somewhere all on one level, and she also told me that she wanted to go and live near Stephen in Tewkesbury. I contacted Stephen with this information, and Stephen found Mum a supported living flat near the river. We drove down there to look at it, and after being shown around by Joan, the manager of Marina Court, Mum asked, "Can I afford to live here?"

"Yes! Of course you can," was my reply.

I stayed with mum for four months to help sell her house and relocate her to the place at Marina Court. It was heavy going, packing up 60 years of living in that house, my childhood home. It was tough choosing what to take and what to put out on the pavement for people to help themselves to. Mum's 'to take' pile, was collected by Stephen, Stephen took Mum that same day. Bar for a mattress for me to sleep on and a kettle, I was left there in an empty house for one night on my own, and it was a very tough emotional night. The next day I closed the front door and pushed the keys through the letter box and didn't look back. Knowing how tough it must have been for me, Lorna breezed in, and took over, whisking me away, and we drove to her house in silence.

When Mum moved into her new flat at Marina Court she became very close to Joan; and Joan was also very supportive of us too! Mum joined every club and activity that was on offer and was very happy there, and she loved to tell her stories of her travels to her new friends.

Mum passed away when she was ninety-three years old after a short illness. Her funeral was held in Tewkesbury Abbey, which she would have been chuffed about. When Mum was diagnosed with leukaemia, Stephen helped her to Skype me. The last thing Mum said to me was, "I'm going on a journey. I'm afraid that you can't come with me this time." **Mum's last day on** this Earth, she was the centre focus of everyone, and Tewksbury Abbey was a very fitting place for her.

Stephen's Eulogy, read by Davin Ginn

I suppose I could begin by saying I have known Mum practically all my life! In common with many others, I have lots of memories of when we were with her. In future days we will have the pleasure of recalling them, but just now I want to speak of Mum, herself.

I think probably the words 'People' and 'Travel' would sum Mum up. She had a deep interest in both. She was very friendly and had no problem approaching complete strangers in a cafe or bus queue, for example. Having a loud voice, it could be a little embarrassing at times when you were with her! However, that led to her having very interesting conversations, both here and all over the world. For example, back in the 1940s Mum worked in a department store called Wards, in Cheltenham. Some years ago, with our late stepfather, she tried to locate the site of the store, which had since been demolished. When she asked two ladies about Ward while in a lift in Cheltenham, they started laughing apparently, Mr. Ward was their grandfather!

Family meant a great deal to Mum. She took a great interest in all her children, grandchildren, and great-grandchildren, *she loved to hear from them, and any news we could give her.*

When we took our problems to Mum (which I often did) she was very supportive. It was instinctive to talk them over with her. *In fact, the day after her passing, I had to stop myself from ringing her to talk about her having just died!*

You would get a wise response from Mum. She was kind and non-judgmental, and if we had *a complaint about someone who was giving us grief, she would see the other person's point of view (annoyingly!).* She showed great empathy for others *and tried to see their point of view and understand* where they were coming from.

She was very generous with what she had. *If money were a problem, she was always willing to help if she could.* For example, "You better talk to your grandma about it" has been her *response on occasion!*

Talking of money, Mum's regard for it was simply that it was for spending! She only saved up so she could go travelling. While our stepdad *was alive, she travelled all round Europe, sometimes in the company of her late sister, Dorothy, and late brother, Ron. She has been to Scotland, Ireland, Belgium,*

Germany, Poland, Slovakia, Austria, Switzerland, Norway, Italy, and Mallorca.

After she was widowed her travel horizons widened to cover the whole world: Canada, Australia, Thailand, and China. She has walked the Wall of China, seen the Niagara Falls in Canada, and cruised the Rhine and Yangtze rivers. When I told Jeremy, my son, she had passed away, he messaged me later and said, "She's always travelling!"

Thailand was special to her because her daughter Christine lives there; Australia was special to her because her grand-daughter, Larissa, lives there; but Canada was a little more special because Fred Chatfield, her oldest brother, who she always looked up to, was honoured there.

Uncle Fred has a street named after him, along with the rest of the crew from the warship, Ajax, which fought in the battle of the River Plate. The town was named Ajax after the ship. When Mum discovered that there was going to be a street naming ceremony, she was determined to be there, even if she had to travel alone.

Mum was pleased and proud to take her daughter, Christine, grand-daughter Lorna and great-grand-daughter, Fleur with her, four generations for the naming ceremony.

Mum had a quiet but strong faith in God. She liked to read her Bible and get along to the local church, of one kind or another, in Luton where she lived. She would attend not only on Sundays, but in the week, too. Eventually, though, we had to move her to a flat here in Tewkesbury when she could no longer manage in her house in Luton. It was remarkable how things just fell into place with the move. Each time she said, "God's looking after me." You will notice that the hymns she requested, and bible reading are all statements of faith. She knew where she was going and who was leading the way.

These last three years at Marina Court were good for Mum. She loved her flat. Being a keen gardener, she loved the beautiful gardens there, too. She had some fuchsias planted there for her - one of her favourite flowers. She also came to love the town of Tewkesbury.

She had a lot of friends in Luton, it was not long before she had a lot of friends here, too, because of her interest in people. She was always grateful for the support and friendship she received.

Mum, your children, your grandchildren, your great-grandchildren, your extended family, and your friends, will all miss you; but thankfully. we have our memories of you to keep in our hearts.

CHAPTER SEVEN

MY EXTENDED FAMILY AND UNCLE FRED

Uncle Fred

Mum's eldest brother, Uncle Fred
Uncle Fred served on HMS Ajax at the battle of the River Plate.

He was mentioned in dispatches.

The Queen Mother and Princess Elisabeth take the salute on HMS Ajax.

Fred was in the navy all his working life, which culminated with him working in the Admiralty. He died 6 months after he retired. Uncle Fred had three children, Joseph, Patsy, and Tony. Sadly, his wife, Nancy, died in childbirth with Tony, and the two older children went to live with Nancy's parents. Tony was brought up by Granny and Aunty Dorothy.

Tony was always a troubled soul, and as a young adult he was admitted into a mental hospital with depression. During this time Tony met his soul mate, Barbara. They got married and had three daughters: Natalie, Isabelle and Nichola, three beautiful girls inside and out! Tragedy struck the family when Barbara, suffering from lupus, committed suicide, leaving Tony with the three young girls. Eventually Tony also committed suicide. His youngest daughter, Nicola was just 12 years old.

I have very fond memories of Tony when we were all children. It gives me pleasure to share these with his daughters. Tony often came to stay with us in Luton. Once after he came with us to a pantomime, he woke up screaming in the night because our cat had jumped on top of him; he thought it was the dragon from the panto. When we were teenagers, Tony came to stay and I can't remember how, but we all got drunk. Tony threw up in the bedroom, but he was too far gone to clear it up before Mum came home, so we all set to, with soapy water and scrubbing brushes.

His fine and beautiful daughters have grown into very fine women, overcoming adversity. Mum and Auntie Dorothy supported Tony's three daughters to get a good education, and they have all been very successful on their chosen paths.

CHAPTER EIGHT

Lorna Jayne

Quite a lot has already been said about Lorna's childhood, her love of horses her teenage years and school. At eighteen, Lorna got a job at the 'Cherries', a residential home for people with learning difficulties. I believe this is where Lorna developed a keen interest in the diversity that life presents us.

When Lorna left that job, she was at an uncomfortable crossroads for a while, but whether she realised it at the time, fate had determined her future. Lorna saw an advert in the *Chichester Observer* for applicants as traffic wardens in Bognor Regis. She soon got an interview, which turned out to be a day- long affair. It started with a ten-stage questionnaire with only ten minutes to answer (some of which seemed ridiculous) and she was struggling to answer them all. The answers were not actually the object of the exercise, which was to put the candidate under pressure! This seemed like an impossible task to Lorna, and it made her angry. The afternoon was set aside for formal interviews before a panel. When Lorna walked in, she simply said, "I do not need an idiot's test to tell me that a car has been parked on a spot for too long." She came home, plonked herself down in a kitchen chair and said to me, "Well...that's one job I won't get." She got the job *and* was the first traffic warden to have a size eight uniform made for her!

Lorna made good friends with the team there. Everything. was hunky dory until, after nearly two years on the job, Lorna saw a poster inviting applicants for a post as a police trainer in equality and diversity. Lorna told the sergeant that she would love to apply but she was, strictly speaking, not a police employee. The sergeant nevertheless encouraged her to go for it. When Lorna pointed out that she was dyslexic and had difficulty filling in forms, he replied, "Don't you think we already know that? They simply cannot turn you down because that would be discrimination!" So, she went for it, and nailed the job!

The position had been created by West Sussex Police as a pilot to address the problems within the force in the aftermath of the Stephen Lawrence murder, an event that brutally exposed racial inequality in British society. Lorna was one of twelve applicants to filter through the initial stages. The candidates were then sent to a residential training facility for a six-week intensive training course in equality and diversity which included one-on-one counselling.

Lorna got the job on a one-year contract which meant that she had to go to various police stations to carry out compulsory training for *all* staff members, from the chief superintendent right down to the car park attendant. Lorna had obviously found her niche in life and loved her job. She found it mind blowing that a lot of people didn't exactly care for the training, simply attended because they *had* to. They had a carefree attitude to what they perceived as a useless waste of their time!

Still, somehow, Lorna soon got them to sit up and take notice. We can only hope! As her contract gradually ended, Lorna remarked to her sergeant friend that she could never go back to being a traffic warden. He skilfully allayed her worries by saying, "Do you really think that after the thousands of pounds spent on your training, the authorities would let that be wasted. Surely you must understand that would not happen?" Sure enough, at the end of her contract Lorna was offered a new post, training the new recruits at Ashford Police Training College.

Whilst Lorna worked there, and due to the very nature of her job, Lorna had good working and personal relations with black high-ranking police officers which eventually guided Lorna to move to the Bramshill training facility in Surrey. Louise and Lorna had already decided to sell their jointly owned house, and having made a decent profit, it gave them both the chance to get on their own property ladder, giving Lorna the financial confidence to buy a small, terraced cottage in Alton, nearer to her workplace.

Lorna became a trainer of the trainers, so to speak, offering help and advice to anyone who needed guidance. As a part of this project, she helped to set up a lesbian police support group. She booked a conference room near Coventry on a set date, sent out flyers and email notifications and then went to the allotted place at the allotted time and waited. She was overwhelmed by the response. She helped them form a group and elect a committee, promising to support them all the way. It was no wonder that Lorna was invited to become Chairperson. However, she smilingly declined, stating that she wasn't gay, but the group would have her total support. Lorna was subsequently invited to attend police conferences in L.A, and New York. Sadly, due to Home-Office funding, or the lack of it, Bramshill was closed, and Lorna was made redundant.

Lorna used her redundancy money to self-fund herself to learn British Sign Language (BSL) and was subsequently asked to be an enabler at the 2012 Para Olympics. She now has the best-ever job working at Treloar Residential School for young people with disability problems, and even with her reduced salary she has no problems compared with the job satisfaction that she now enjoys. Nowadays, she wears two hats:

trainer of staff in equality and diversity, and enabler to the students, to source recreational/educational extra-curricular activities.

Lorna has just celebrated her 10-year anniversary with her partner, Donovan, along with two Rhodesian ridgeback dogs and a miniature dachshund.

Lorna has maintained her riding and has been very successful with her first "owned" horse, Lulu, a huge (17.2 hands high) horse. Lulu became Lorna's horse by chance. The people who owned her couldn't manage her, and Lorna got her for a knock down price. Oh boy! She was a troubled horse. However, Lorna got to grips with her, finding that 'work' and training was needed to satisfy this work hungry horse. Lorna competed with Lulu to advanced level dressage.

Lorna once told me that she found Lulu a difficult horse to love. Lulu's temperament was questionable, however she loved to 'work'; it was in the stable that you had to be careful. At the age of 12 years, Lulu became seriously lame, and the decision to euthanize her, although difficult, was the only thing to do. Lulu would have hated being **turned out in a** field and not worked. Anyone reading this will understand that these decisions are not made lightly. When you take animals into your life, they become your family and your responsibility. That horrible day, Lorna was taken out by a friend, just to take her mind off Lulu.

By chance, Lorna saw a 3-year-old, very well-bred horse that had a very kind and sweet nature, and she couldn't put this horse out of her mind. In the end Lorna bought her. Having never owned a young horse that was unbroken Lorna was very worried that she might spoil her by doing it wrong, but with help "Just Dance," pet named "Tutu", was quietly and gently introduced to saddle, bridle, and rider. Tutu is a spirited young horse, without any malice in her. She hasn't been without some physical problems; however, with the best horse hospital in the south of England and good insurance it's all worked out.

Unlike Lulu before her, she is an easy horse to take care of. She is now building back up to continue with her dressage training. Now, Lorna and Tutu are enjoying hacking out along the country lanes.

Lorna with Lulu

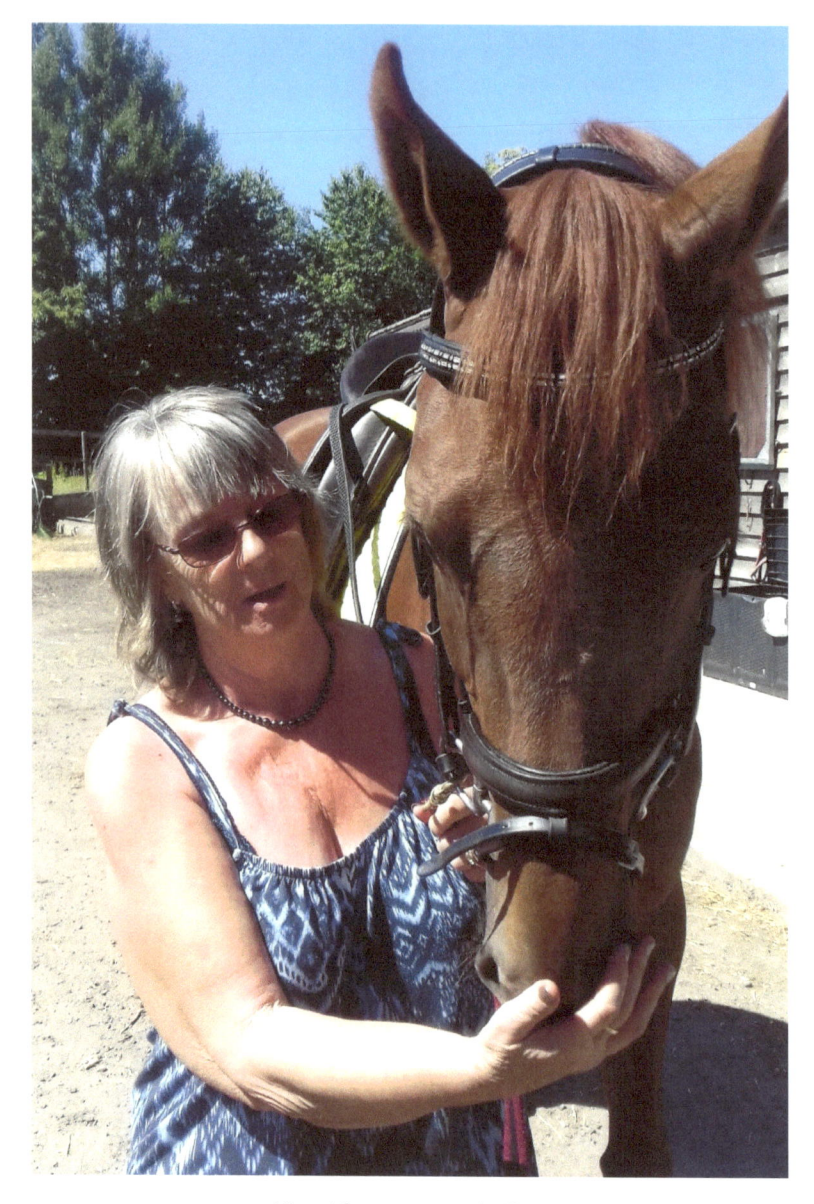

Me with sweet gentle Tutu

Lorna in the competitor's marquee at Brighton Driving Trial when she was eighteen years old.

*Me, Donovan, and Lorna
New Year's Eve supper out in Phuket*

*Lorna and Donovan at the 2012 Olympic Park,
Lorna wearing her Olympic uniform with pride.*

THE DUKE OF EDINBURGH AND I

About us.

We love dogs and Bluebells. Me with Robyn

Lorna loves blue bells in the woods with Robyn.

*Mum loves dogs and blue bells.
In the woods with Ruby*

*Lou with Boris and Bella in the woods
Our whole family love,
dogs and bluebells in the wood*

Lou with Boris, Keeper, and Bella

CHAPTER NINE

Louise May

In 1970 we made the decision to complete our family, and on August 13th at 10 pm, my second daughter, Louise May was born. Mum was present at the birth of Louise when she was delivered by my midwife in the bedroom of our bungalow in Allotment Road. Mum had come over to the Isle of Wight to help me for the first week. Louise was always known to me as Lou, but Mum's middle name was May, so Louise became Louise May. Since Lorna was born in Mum's house, and she was present at Louise's birth they both shared a deep bond with their Nana.

Lou grew up to be mad about all animals. When we had our Irish setter, 'Honey,' and our whippet, Lou used to get into their box and sleep with them. She was such a funny girl; she would scramble around the kitchen floor to grab the dog biscuits that I tossed down to the dogs. When Lou was eighteen months old, Honey had a litter of puppies, and Lou spent hours playing with them. Lou was at her happiest when she was with animals. Mmmm, I wonder where she got that from?

Lou Learnt to ride when she was very young; almost before she could walk! She loved just sitting on a pony, and inevitably I brought one of the ponies (Dillan) into the garden for her. She would sit on it while I was doing the housework; no need for a babysitter or a play pen. Another one of my ponies, Kestrel, gave birth to a foal in the back garden. It was a surprise, so we named her foal Maverick. When Maverick was about 2 months old, because it was a lovely sunny day, what else could we do, but lead Kestrel and her foal down the road. Lorna led Kestrel with Lou sitting on top, bare back! I followed behind to take cine film!

Maverick ran loose down the road. Most of the street had got used to seeing these occurrences It was so funny to see Kestrel trotting, Lou bobbing up and down, her hand full of mane and giggling her head off; funny but also dangerous. Growing up without fear for myself, I never feared for my children either. No hard hat and she was wearing a dress; Lorna was only five at the time.

Lou was a quiet and loving little girl who always looked as if she was thinking. Lorna often used to speak for Lou! If I asked Lou a question, Lorna would give me the answer. Lorna was the opposite, a cocky in-your-face chatterbox.

It was a complete rarity for it to snow on the Isle of Wight, but when it did, we made the most of it. We all went for a toddle up the lane; Lou was all wrapped up in her red duffle coat and white wellies, wearing a green bonnet knitted by me. To make sure that she didn't get cold hands, I put plastic bags on top of her mittens. Lou slipped up on the ice, and struggled to stand up again, but her determined nature shone through.

1973 – those were happy days with lots of dogs and ponies. Lou went to the village nursery school when she was three years old. Those happy days slowly disappeared to turn into difficult ones as my marriage disintegrated. September 1974 and Lou loved her ducklings and my Wendy house caravan; despite its cramped interior, we enjoyed our Sunday time together. Two months later, in November, Lou and Lorna moved into the caravan with me. I felt secure in the knowledge that Lou enjoyed her new, Wendy-house home, playing with the ducks in open spaces. Mostly we all enjoyed the peaceful, pressure-free atmosphere that now surrounded us.

Although we were on the waiting list for a council house, in the end we couldn't wait any longer and the three of us moved over to Woodend at Easter, 1975. It was fantastic to be joined by our 5-year-old Irish Setter, Honey—my Mum had looked after her until we were more settled, and we had all missed her. I've already told you that one morning Lou wandered down looking for me and was knocked over and bitten on her cheek by Miss Broad's two Doberman dogs. They also tried to fight with Honey, but she stood her ground and the Dobermans, being cowards, backed off. Miss Broad just casually said to us was, 'you were warned!'

Later, Lou and Lorna were enrolled into the West Ashling village school. Life at Woodend was certainly very different; it was in the middle of a wood, and miles from any local shops. However, Lorna and Lou seemed to like it there. In 1976 I met my future second husband, Richard, a farm worker, and as our relationship developed, we eventually moved into Pitlands farm cottage with him.

Lou and Lorna flourished on the farm, where they could play in the fields and hay barn. The farm reared calves so Lou and Lorna enjoyed seeing these young calves that were kept in a large barn through the winter. In the spring the calves were released out into the open fields, and it was all hands to the deck. Lou was thrilled to see them all galloping and leaping about in the meadow.

As soon as we were settled, Alpha came over from Woodend, and she slept in the garden shed. After school, Lorna and Lou took Alpha out for a ride in the woods, then grazed her on the grass verges, and we were given hay from the farm to feed her.

At this time Lou was attending Compton village school. Both girls were picked up from the farm and taken to school in a minibus. It worried me that Lou's education was not the best, having constantly moved schools. It was suggested to me that she would be better off attending a school in Chichester, as she was struggling with reading and writing. That was very upsetting, and I blamed myself. In the summer holidays, I arranged for Lou to have some private tuition in reading and writing, and I'm glad that I did as this wonderful lady teacher diagnosed that Lou was dyslexic. Lorna and Lou were both left-handed, which contributed to them both being dyslexic, something I had never heard of before. It was called 'mirror writing'—words appeared to be back-wards and upside down. Lorna told me that when she went to the village school on the Isle of Wight the teacher used to tie her left hand to the chair and force her to write with her right hand! This provided me with deep thoughts; what else did I not know? I informed the school, and Lou never looked back, making excellent progress in senior school.

We spent many happy days driving the ponies around the UK, and Lou was always my groom, the obvious choice. She was the perfect person to do this as she knew the ponies well and they trusted her. Lou came with us to the party nights in the marquee and had the freedom to run around with the other drivers' children, in and out of the marquee, which was great. When we competed in

France and Belgium, Lou was always my groom during the dressage and cones phase; she was excellent at it.

When Lou was thirteen years old, as a surprise we bought her a whippet puppy from one of my carriage driving friends, Louise Sargent. Annabel was her name, and I kept her hidden from sight beside me until Lou came home. Lou was over the moon, and Annabel was whisked up to bed with Lou, forming an inseparable life-long relationship. Annie eventually passed over the rainbow bridge when she was sixteen years old.

Lou's best friend, Louise Saunders, rode Nick Brook's horse at Boxgrove. Louise was 16 years old, Lou was 14 years old, and they were just like sisters. Louise had grown up in Hong Kong with her father who was the manager of the Happy Valley racetrack. Louise's mother lived in Australia. Louise was a very accomplished horse rider and she competed in the Asian Games. She was spotted by an English horse trainer and came to live in England.

Louise and Lou spent many hours up at Boxgrove, playing with the horses. It wasn't long before Louise came to live with us in the council house in Westerton, where I had been rehoused after being evicted from the farm cottage. Louise coached Lou and offered to sell her a horse, Bandit. Buying Bandit for Lou for £800, was a sinch. Lou had a lot of fun with Bandit, doing cross country events and a bit of show jumping. Bandit proved to be an excellent jumping horse and was sold on to a show jumper. After Bandit was sold, Lou started to ride Nick Brook's horse under the watchful eye of her adopted trainer, Louise. He was called 'Phineas Finn,' pet named Finn, and at 17 hands he was a massively tall horse. Nick had inherited this horse when his mother died but as Nick didn't ride, Lou, with help from Louise, shared him. Louise evented him, and Lou started to ride him side-saddle.

Nick Brook's and Boxgrove competition stables.

Nick was a huge friend of mine. He owned the stables where I kept my horses. Nick was very enthusiastic about what we did. He came with us to Waregem in Belgium. While I slept in the caravan, Nick and Lou slept in the lorry with the rain beating down on the roof all night like the sound of a drum. Despite that we were all in high spirits.

Nick came to my rescue when the time came to say goodbye to Robin; he invited Robin to spend his last days in the field that he knew so well, and then oversaw Robin's departure. Robin's ashes are buried alongside Finn's ashes on the farm. Nick was tragically killed in a car crash on an icy road just before Christmas, December 21st, 2007. He was just 54 years old and is missed very much by many people.

Lou left school at 15 and got a job on a government youth training scheme, for which she was paid a fixed wage of £27 a week. Respectfully, Lou gave me £10 for her keep and £10 for Bandit's keep, leaving her with £7. From that she managed to save up to buy herself a second-hand moped.

(*At this point it needs to be said that when I got my* first *job I earned £1.10s a week, and out of that I gave Mum the 10s for my keep. Having been brought up in the belief that nothing in this life is free, my daughters followed my lead.*)

With Lou's trusty moped came independence. She could whiz to work and then whiz to the stables at very little expense; Lou's needs were few. She was working as an office junior at Blades helicopter school at Goodwood Airfield which was only five minutes away from home. After a couple of years, Blades expanded into fixed wing aircraft. Lou was asked to set up the new office. She had truly found her feet. One of her daily jobs was to go to the control tower to collect the weather forecast. She was then headhunted by the control tower to go there to work, which she did.

Lou flourished, getting quite cheeky with the pilots. A stunt pilot dared Lou to go up in his stunt plane with him, What! Lou hitched up her skirt and got right in. During her work at the control tower Lou met a helicopter pilot, Nick. There was a spark straight away. Nick was her first and only boyfriend; they started dating, and once flew to Paris for a weekend. Nick sometimes took Lou with him in the helicopter to London when he had to go there on company business. Protocol meant that they had to fly along the route of the river Thames. When Lou was 20 years old, she and Nick got engaged. For Lou's 21st birthday we all went to the horse racing at Fontwell and had lunch in the dining room there. Lou is a very strong racing fan.

In September 1992 Lou and Nick were married. In my eyes this was a fairy tale wedding. The service was held in Boxgrove Priory. We were driven from the priory in a carriage pulled by our family's ponies, including Alpha who was a 27-year-old at the time. A dear friend of mine, Mike Higlet, a well-established horse team driver drove the newlyweds to the reception in the ballroom of Goodwood House, which was complimentary because both Lou and Nick worked at Goodwood airfield.

The finale was when a helicopter flew over Goodwood house. The pilot was told off about that, but too late, the deed was done. Lou and Nick flew off to Amberly castle for the first night of their honeymoon. Pre the wedding Lou and Nick had moved to Shannon on the west coast of Ireland. At that time Nick was working in search and rescue. Unable to work because Lou was English, not Irish, Lou needed some way to fill her time while Nick was working. She located a horse sales yard, and the owner offered Lou a ride whenever she wanted. Going home smelling 'horsey' was not the best idea. Lou told me that these horses were kept in poor conditions; they stood knee deep in manure as they didn't have enough staff to clear out the stables.

Nick and Lou bought a Pyrenean Mountain dog puppy, so that Lou could take up dog showing. And in 1993 no-one was more thrilled than me, with the news that Lou and Nick were expecting their first baby.

Fleur was born on July 6th, 1994, in the hospital in Limerick. Naturally, that changed many things. Nick had been heading up some dangerous rescues in the Atlantic Ocean, but now he decided that for the sake of his family—Lou and his daughter Fleur—he wanted a nine to five job. He found one flying out to the oil rigs in the North-Sea from Aberdeen. Lou, Nick, and Fleur moved to Inverurie near Aberdeen, and bought a house off plan. However, Bristow's helicopters had other ideas and sent Nick out to Stornoway, in the Outer Hebrides for two years, doing search and rescue again!

This gave me the opportunity to stay with Lou, Nick, and Fleur twice, flying to Stornoway from Inverness. Once I took my mother, and we went on the ferry from Ullapool. Lou took Nana out with her when she walked Dillan, sometimes along the cliff tops, and the views of the North Atlantic were amazing. Nick took us out in the search and rescue helicopter while he was taking part in a search and rescue exercise. He dropped all three of us on the side of a mountain we were his guineapigs. Nick flew off, then came back to pick us up. Lou had to be discrete about whether we were able to go out in the helicopter just in case a real rescue was needed.

Once Nick was asked to circumnavigate the Isle of Lewis for an ordinance survey. We were flying low and one of his crew asked me to go and sit with my feet dangling out the side door, which was great and exciting. Of course, I was well and truly strapped in.

Sadly, through no fault of their own, Lou's marriage didn't survive. Lou and Fleur moved down to Sussex to live with me until permanent arrangements were made. Nick was a very good father who adored Fleur. Lou was tasked with searching for a new home, but all the houses near me were very expensive. The solution came from out of the blue—sell my three-bed house to Lorna and Lou jointly, Nick's share being held in trust for Fleur. I didn't need three bedrooms now and this set Lorna and Lou onto the property ladder.

Lou has an amazing affinity with dogs and is an exceptional dog trainer. She started with a black labrador she named Otto. Otto came from a long line of field trial championship dogs. Lou trained Otto up to do field trials, and as a team, they had a lot of success. Otto was a very special dog. Lou had bought him as a puppy and had loads of fun with him. He lived a very full and active life until he unexpectedly died of a brain tumour, which broke Lou's heart.

After a while, being dogless was not an option for Lou, so she decided to 'have another go' at showing dogs. She bought a cocker spaniel, named Keeper, for showing. Tragedy struck, when Keeper, at a very young age, became very unwell. His illness was very unusual and difficult to diagnose, and he was referred to a specialist at great expense (luckily Keeper was insured) and after many months of treatment he was stabilized. But then, to complicate matters, Keeper was diagnosed as being allergic to some proteins, and later became diabetic. Now, with careful management and daily insulin, he is a happy boy.

Lou is a naturally quiet and private person, but she never ceases to amaze me with her dare devil side. She treated herself to a sky dive/parachute drop for one of her birthdays. In 1970, the year Lou was born, the first ever open-air rock festival/concert was held on the Isle of Wight. On Lou's fortieth birthday she and her friend went to the rock festival/concert again and camped in a tent! It reminded me of my family camping days.

Lou is now the bed manager for mental health services and has her own house, two rag doll cats, Princess and Coco, Keeper, the cocker spaniel, two whippets, Boris (Cobyco City Limits) and Bella (Cobyco Cover Queen). Lou has done very well showing her whippets, qualifying for Crufts with Bella, so naturally she entered. Where Bella was placed is irrelevant; she got there!

Boris, a stunning looking boy, was given to Lou by his breeder, Lynne, with whom Lou had become friends after buying Bella, and proving herself to be a good show/home owner. Due to covid, Boris, along with loads of other promising puppies, missed all the puppy show classes. He has just come into his own and has qualified for Crufts 2023. To Top all this off, Lou is the proud part-owner of three racehorses in a syndicate. Since writing this Lou has acquired a fourth racehorse.

I am very proud of Lou and her many achievements.

CHRISTINE SUSAN MAY

Lou age 4 with her duckling

Lou field trialling with Otto

Me and Mum in the Helicopter.

Mum, and I waiting to board.

THE DUKE OF EDINBURGH AND I

My groom

Lou in Iceland at the hot springs

Up, up, and away, sky diving.

CHAPTER TEN

Fleur May

The 6th of July 1994 was the day when I became a grandmother. My granddaughter, Fleur, was born in Limerick Hospital. I was at work when the news came, and my boss gave me the evening off, sending me home, as I was unable to concentrate.

I flew over to Shannon when Fleur was three weeks old, and she was the dearest, sweetest, little girl. Right from the start she was the apple of everyone's eye. Staying with the 'new parents' for two weeks was the best time ever for me. All too soon I had to fly back to work. The next time we met, was at Fleur's christening, aged 5 months. Unable to help myself, I found myself talking to Fleur in baby language as one did in my youth, but I was soon asked to speak properly to her and quit the high-pitched squeaky voice. Fleur was so adorable. Truthfully, I have never seen Fleur cry and from a very early age she always struck me as being deeply in thought; she would study things and people with intent, or gaze out of the window, deep in thought. I always wondered what was on her mind.

Fleur was a very active child, and rarely, if ever, did she allow herself to be pushed in a pushchair. Instead, she'd be running along in front with the dog, or running on an empty beach, of which there are many in Ireland. The family pets were a huge Pyrenean Mountain dog called Dillon, Archie the black cat, and Jasper the Somalian cat. Fleur gathered up Dillon's fur as Lou brushed him, and she used it to stroke her face with it, especially at bedtime, when she would go to sleep with a fist full of Dillon's fur in her hand. Eventually, whenever I asked what I could buy for Fleur, I'd be told to buy her a bag of cotton wool balls, so that she could be weaned off Dillon's fur! Oh, my word! How thrilled Fleur was with them.

Fleur was half the size of Dillon, but she used to hold his lead on beach walks. He was a very gentle dog, originally used to guard flocks of sheep, but now Dillon guarded Fleur instead.

When Fleur was 18 months old, she stayed with me while Lou and Nick had a week away. This slightly concerned me, as circumstances dictated that Fleur did not know me very well, and I was worried that she might fret. None of it! She was such a well-adjusted and confident little girl; she obviously felt very safe in her world. She was so adaptable. When Fleur moved in with me, I asked Lou if Fleur had a pushchair, but was most certainly told not, that she walked everywhere properly. And so she did! Every day, twice a day, we walked the whippets (all five of them), and Fleur ran up the front with them; she never seemed to get tired.

In the week Fleur was with me she didn't cry once. She had a small photo album with photos of her Mum, Dad, Dillon the dog, and Archie, and Jasper, the cats. Before bed Fleur looked through the album kissing them all good night.

Apparently, Fleur occasionally sleep-walked. I'd never experienced anything like that before! One evening, alarmingly, Fleur suddenly appeared in the sitting room with a strange expression on her face and no response when I spoke to her. Under instructions given to me by Lou and Nick about this, I simply, just turned her around and walked her back upstairs to bed!

Fleur's Dad.

While Nick worked in search and rescue from Shannon Airport, he took part in a very difficult and dangerous rescue. He was called out one night to fly out into the Atlantic Ocean to a stricken Spanish trawler. The sea had waves 20 metres high, and the wind was gusting. While the crew were in the middle of winching the trawlermen up into the helicopter. the winch cable suddenly got caught in the wheelhouse and snapped, whipping up and damaging the rota blades! Nick made an instant decision to abandon his winchman and the Spaniards not yet onboard, to save the helicopter and all the people on board from catastrophe. He successfully landed the damaged helicopter in Galway. The RAF collected the winchman and remaining ship's crew. Nick was recognized for his swift action, but this rescue formed part of the deciding factor to change jobs and re-locate to Aberdeen.

The family moved to Inverurie, and then almost immediately were relocated to Stornoway; not what Nick had in mind. Fleur seemed to be oblivious to whizzing around the country to various new homes. She was very secure in her life, very happy and confident.

Fleur went to nursery school in Stornoway. Fleur's teacher there had grey hair, so Fleur referred to her as the Grey Lady. Fleur always referred to her grandfather as Man. When I visited them all in Stornoway, taking my mother with me, this presented Fleur with a dilemma—what to call this new lady in her life and where this newcomer fitted into her world. She put her thinking cap on—that is Mum, that is Nana, so she settled on Great Grandma.

One morning Fleur went into Great Grandma's bedroom and saw a packet of sweets. She immediately announced that she wanted one. Nick who was close by, gently corrected her saying, "Fleur, you don't say I <u>want</u> one, you say I <u>need</u> one." Fleur's brain thought it over, and out came these words, "Great Grandma I need; I want a sweet! please". Fleur, only 4 years old, was such a funny little girl, thinking things through before coming out with some wonderful comments.

When Lou and Nick relocated to Scotland, the extensive car journey with the dog and cat (Archie had passed away) were deemed to be too long for Fleur. So, she moved back into my house temporarily until Lou and Nick were settled. Just a few days, then, flying from Gatwick to Aberdeen with my precious grandchild; it felt like an honour, to be entrusted to carry out this task. I have always told Fleur that she was my favourite granddaughter, and she always laughs at me saying, "That is because I am your only granddaughter!" She now calls me 'Titchy' because she is taller than me!

Lou and Nick made sure Fleur experienced as many things as possible in her formative years, making sure that she was rounded and would be able to make informed choices well in life. She learned how to ride, swim, ski, play the piano, and strum a tune on a guitar (Nick is very musical and plays the piano and guitar). She tried drama classes, and dance and she became accomplished at judo, and is a very talented singer. Nick and Fleur recorded Fleur singing 'Le vie en Rose' and it is the most beautiful thing I have ever heard. I took a copy to my Mum for her to listen to. Mum knew immediately that it was Fleur singing, and she loved it. This recording was played in Tewkesbury Abbey at Mum's funeral.

Nick wanted Fleur to have a private education, but Lou felt sure that Fleur would benefit enormously if she went to the lovely little village school in Westergate. It was charming to see Fleur in her school uniform the day she started school. She flourished there, was well thought of, and was chosen several times to befriend new girls at school. She loved to read, and her nose was always buried in a book. She read them fast, too, so much so, that I didn't think she was really reading them until she told me what the story was all about.

Later, when Lou's marriage broke down and she moved nearer to me, Lou worked while Fleur was at the junior school and it was up to me to collect Fleur from school, and to take her home for tea. After tea, Fleur would look out of the window to see when Glen, who was then my husband, was driving in. When he arrived, Fleur ran around like a headless chicken looking for somewhere to hide. Her favourite places were under the coffee table or behind my voile curtains. She was clearly visible in both places, but she still asked me, "Can you see me?" Glen would come in through the door sniffing, and saying in a creepy voice, "I can smell children," imitating the fictional 'child catcher,' in the

Chitty, chitty bang bang story. He would look all around the flat while she giggled.

Another of my favourite poems by AA. Milne, that Mum used to recite to me was "The stair where I sit". There is a staircase leading up to my apartment, and one day Fleur and I sat on the middle stair so that she could listen to my rendition of the poem for her.

> *Halfway down the stairs is the stair where I sit,*
> *there is not another stair quite like it,*
> *it isn't at the bottom, it isn't at the top,*
> *but this is the stair where I always stop.*
> *Halfway down the stairs isn't up, and it isn't down.*
> *It isn't in the nursery, it isn't in the town,*
> *all sorts of funny thoughts run round my head,*
> *It isn't anywhere! It's somewhere else instead!*

Fleur was captivated by this poem, as was I when Mum used to recite it to me so many years ago.

She was such a cuddly little girl, and she would snuggle up to me, but in some ways was quite gullible. She loved fairies, and in her collection of books was one about fairies. Our garden had a huge holm oak tree with snow drops and crocuses under it in the springtime, and I used to tell Fleur this is where the fairies lived. A suggestion from me? I would say, "Take your book down to the fairy garden and read to them, and one might just come out." And off she would go, story book in hand, but sorry to say, Fleur never saw a fairy.

An opportunity arose for me to take Fleur to Lapland to see the 'real' Father Christmas. The night before we went Fleur slept on a mattress in my apartment, we had to wake up at 4am to go to Gatwick and from that moment on the trip was magical. The plane was full of grandparents accompanied by excited children. The cabin crew were all dressed as fairies or gnomes. Landing in Lapland was a fairy story come true.

First stop was for me to be fitted out with thermal clothing; Fleur already had her own skiing onesie. Most of the children rushed off to see Father Christmas, but we went to see the reindeer instead, and went for a ride in a sleigh. Then off we went to see Father Christmas. He was a huge man dressed in a traditional Lapland outfit, and he also had a proper full and long beard! Fleur sat next to him, and he asked her, "What would you like for Christmas". Fleur's answer was, an "S Club 7 CD." Santa whispered that information to me, he asked her what else she wanted.

"Nothing."

What? No dolly or doll's pram?

"No, nothing else thank you."

Throughout the day there was only one hour of darkness, so everywhere was lit by candles in the snow, making it very enchanting! We went to see the husky puppies, and afterwards had a husky sledge ride. As we climbed into the sledge, I noticed that it was anchored to a pine tree, the Huskies were jumping about eager to go, and yelping, a wonderful sound in the pine forest. Once we were safely seated, with a reindeer skin as a blanket, the anchor was removed, and off we flew at high speed along a candle-lit track. It was thrilling.

In the centre of the village there was an ice slide. It was made of a huge pile of ice with steps each side chipped out of the ice. Fleur joined the Lapland children who lived in the village climbing up and sliding down. All too soon it was time for our return flight to England. Fleur was back in her own bed by midnight. Sweet dreams, Fleur.

One of my favourite singers is Russell Watson, and he has a song called 'Winter Wonderland'. His words are a perfect memory for me of that day.

> *Wake up, wake up, your sleepy head,*
> *get up, get up, get out of bed,*
> *we're going to a winter wonderland".*

When she was 11, Fleur moved to the comprehensive school, just five minutes away from my apartment. She thrived there, too, passing all her exams with very high marks. At her leaving prom dance she was voted Prom Queen by all her peers.

I took Fleur to see her great grandmother one day and her great uncle Stephen came round to visit. He noticed that Fleur was wearing a long baggy jumper full of holes. Stephen remarked in amazement, "Fleur your jumper is full of holes." She replied, "Never mind, it's my favourite jumper." Fleur was not one for high fashion or 'labels,' she always wears what she likes.

Fleur wanted to do a degree in human conflict, she enrolled at Leeds University., where she attained her PhD with Honors. This path led Fleur into the world of refugees. While Fleur was studying, she worked as a volunteer for the Leeds Refugee Counsel, and this gave her a bigger insight into human conflict issues. Instead of taking a year out Fleur went to Maastricht University in Holland to continue her studies.

During Fleur's uni. summer break, Fleur spent 6 weeks in China as a volunteer, helping to organize a summer camp for the children of several schools. The group of volunteers travelled to several schools, promoting the summer camp. Fleur told me that she had sung to 2000 children in a huge open parade ground. The children filled this massive parade ground in class groups. The object of the summer camp was to put on a show. This included teaching the children how to make outfits, props and background sets. The theme of the show was 'Harry Potter' and it was a massive success. At the end of the six weeks, Nick flew out to join Fleur for a week to see a little bit of China!

Nowadays, Fleur has a brilliant soulmate in her life, Robbie. Luckily, Robbie is a lover of cats, too. Together they have two cats, brother, and sister; no worries they have both been spayed.

Fleur and Robbie made a surprise visit to me here in Phuket. That day, I'd been given the task to go to the airport to pick up 'a guest'. Oh wow! It was Fleur and Robbie who appeared, walking out to meet me! I was blown away. What a wonderful time I had, having them there for two whole weeks. All too soon they had to fly back home to work.

Fleur's part time job, at the refugee council in Leeds, was to source housing, schooling, doctors, and interpreters for the refugees. Following on from her PhD, Fleur wanted to do her master's in law, (especially in relation to refugee status). To help with this aim, she had spent a week's work experience at a solicitor's firm in Leeds, and that experience set her thoughts onto working as a solicitor. She saw an advert for a job with a national firm of lawyers and applied, went through stringent interviews until finally she was offered the job. The solicitors offered to sponsor Fleur to do a higher qualification which would enable her to be a practicing solicitor and have a contract with them when she finished. She passed her first set of exams for her master's degree with distinction and will soon get her final exam results. Fleur started her new job this September. There are no words that can describe how proud I am of my 'favourite granddaughter'.

Fleur with Great Grandma

In 2018 Fleur, Lorna, and Lou had a girly holiday going to an African game reserve, a riding holiday, no less. Good job that Fleur had learned the basics of horse riding as a child. Under the umbrella of Lou and Aunty Lorna, all three went out daily with two African guides to see the wildlife. They swam with the horses in a waterhole/lake, which was great fun for all. At the end of each day, a Land Rover would arrive with canapés and drinks, which they had while watching the sunset. The horses were relieved of their saddles and bridles and turned loose in the bush for the night. Lorna, Lou, and Fleur travelled back to camp in the Land Rover. Drinks and supper were then followed by a swim in the pool. Sure enough, the horses were waiting outside the stables in the morning for their breakfast.

If I was asked to describe Fleur this is what I would say: 5'4" with long dark hair, an intoxicating laugh, and a beautiful smile. Fleur has grown up to be a beautiful person inside and out, but she has her feet firmly grounded thanks to her Mum and Dad. She is incredibly modest and thoughtful of others.

Fleur follows in our footsteps with her love of animals, especially cats. She and Robbie have bought a home together in the suburbs of Leeds, and as every fairytale book end, she is living "happily ever after".

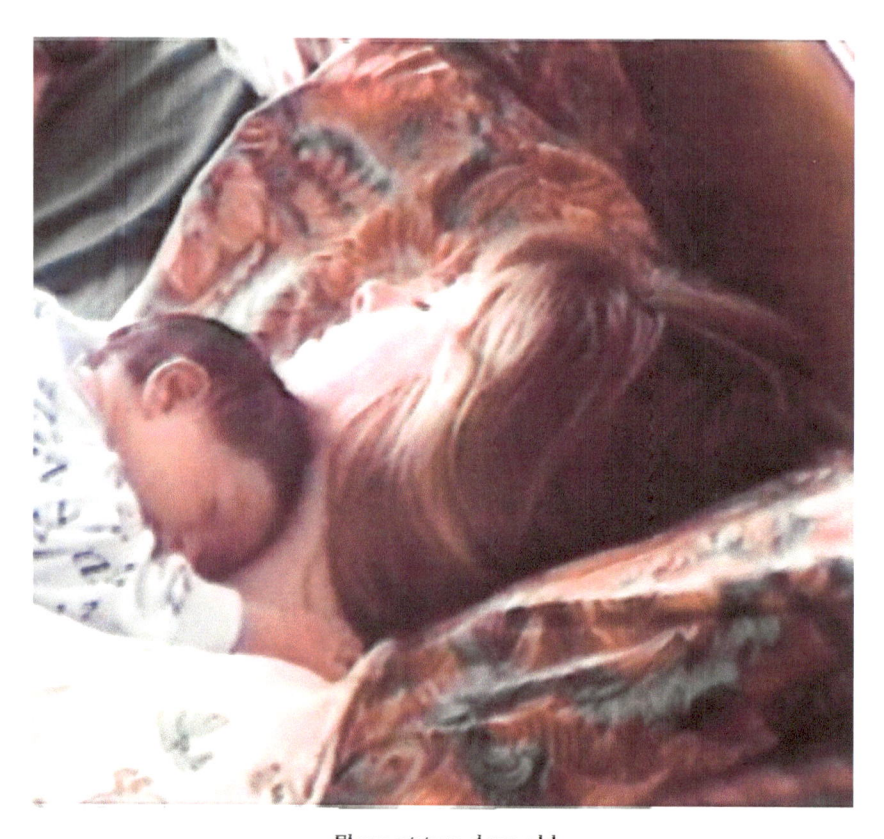

Fleur at two days old

THE DUKE OF EDINBURGH AND I

Fleur with Dillan

Fleur, Lou, and Aunty Lorna in Africa

Happy families
Fleur with Boris, Keeper, and Bella

Fleur with Tamarind
When she stayed with me in my house in Thailand

Cat lover, Fleur with Lou's cat, Coco

Graduation Day

Surprise, surprise!
Fleur and Robbie arriving here.

CHAPTER ELEVEN

MY BIG BROTHER STEPHEN

Stephen Bernard was born in Eastbourne on Wednesday, May 31st, 1944. Mum told me that he was a very cute and gentle child. She also told me that Stephen had chosen my middle name, Susan, because even at the tender age of 4years old he was very keen on a little girl down the road named Susan. After my birth, Stephen went out to pick a bunch of wild flowers to give to Mum.

Mum prayed that Stephen would not be born on a Wednesday because according to the rhyme, 'Wednesday's child is full of woe'. That does seem to sum up Stephen; he has always had the weight of the world on his shoulders, taking on other people's troubles, sometimes personal, otherwise a taxi driver on demand or to fix things. Over the years Stephen has helped me no end, which makes me forever grateful.

Stephen was born with blonde hair which later turned black although I don't remember this happening. Stephen was a very kind and gentle boy, and I confess that as his teenage sister I saw that side of him as a sign of weakness. Stephen grew tall very quickly, and eventually he grew to be 6ft with a very slim build. He had never worn jeans; it was always long trousers. When he finally did start wearing jeans, he insisted that Mum iron a crease down the front.

He was a gentleman in every sense of the word, he was meticulous with everything. He always held his cutlery, plate, and glass up to the light to make sure they were shiny and clean, he even had his own cutlery! Stephen was also very articulate; he once said to me that swearing is a sign of a limited vocabulary That made me very cross, which drove me to make up the following sentence, which flew out of my mouth at him: 'If you think that I should tolerate such diabolical insolence from you, you unsophisticated piece of animosity, you are wrong!' Tossing my nose up in the air, I strutted off, being the snotty horrible girl that I became at times. If someone told me, you cannot, I will, I did and I would.

Stephen's pride and joy was a Norton motorbike that he kept spotless. He took to it to pieces just so that he could remove any unnecessary parts to make the motor bike lighter. Once he took me for a ride on the back and he drove at 90 miles an hour. It didn't frighten me; it was thrilling.

Being ever the perfectionist, Stephen took his advanced motor bike and car tests which were run by the police in those days. Most weekends Stephen spent hours washing and polishing his motor bike. Once, as he stood back to admire it a stray dog wandered onto our drive and cocked its leg on the front wheel. Stephen rushed into the house shouting, "A dog just peed on my bike!" This was the first time we'd ever heard a swear word uttered by Stephen.

Having a lifelong passion for motorbikes, Stephen bought a customised motorbike that was pink. This was the colour of the previous owner, who was a bike racer. Stephen bought himself pink leathers and helmet to match. His last bike was a Honda Fireblade, which he only rode out on Sundays or special occasions, but he eventually gave it up through lack of riding opportunities

Stephen was naturally a keen gliding enthusiast, too. At the age of sixteen, he learned to fly at the London Gliding Club under Dad's watchful eye. At Stephen's first solo flight, the whole family attended, even Mum. We all held our breath when the cable broke during the assent, but he handled it like a professional and landed safely.

After I got married, Stephen asked me what it was like. My reply—'anything is better than living here'. But I hadn't realized that Stephen had fallen for the dentist's receptionist! Barbara played cupid and organized for them to meet. She had noticed that the mere mention of her brother's name made Marilynne blush and giggle. After a fairly short courtship Stephen became a member of the Plymouth Brethren congregation, of which Marilynne's father was the pastor. Stephen was baptised into that faith, and subsequently carried a bible with him everywhere. Remember my time at the Pentecostal Church? Please do not try to convert me!

Amazingly, Stephen failed to get into Luton Grammar School. All his basic education was at Denbigh Road Secondary School. On leaving school, Stephen got a job working for the British Air Corporation (BAC) in Bedford. They sponsored him to get his degree in aircraft science and he studied for three years on block release to get his BSc from Sussex University.

Stephen and Marilynne lived partly in Brighton and partly in Bedford. They became a family when their first child was born, a son named Christopher, soon followed by Jeremy. Later on, Sarah and David joined the family. Stephen is a very loving family man although sometimes he got stressed with holding down a tough and responsible job, with 4 children under 6 years of age.

Stephen is a very clever man and qualified as a scientist, working for BAC, Smiths Industries and Airbus. Later, under the MOD, Stephen worked on the Harrier jump jet, and latterly the Airbus A380. After Mum flew out to Australia in the A380 Airbus, Mum told Stephen, "Next time you work on an aircraft design, please make the toilets bigger!"

Stephen worked for ten years on a top-secret project to develop a guided landing system to use in poor visibility. Stephen and his team travelled around to demonstrate it in Saudi Arabia and Seattle. Finally, it was launched at Cape Canaveral alongside another system that was being developed by the USA. Afterwards, the Russians bought the American system and Stephen was made redundant overnight, even escorted off the premises. A dreadful thing to happen after ten years of service.

Below is a breakdown of Stephens resume.

- An aerospace engineer with a wide-ranging experience of avionic system development.
- An initiative-taking individual who enjoys working with people as a team player, or in a liaison role with other teams, customers, and suppliers. SC cleared.
- *(SC clearance is the most common form of security clearance in the UK. Being SC cleared is a requirement for any role that involves frequent access to documents classified as secret, or occasional supervised access to top secret files in government or defence organizations.)*

Stephen had a very full career in aviation. He tried to retire but was asked to stay on as a consultant. When Stephen did eventually retire, he confided to me that the day he walked out of work for the last time, years of knowledge and experience went with him!

During this time Stephen's marriage failed, and Marilynne took the children with her to Northampton. Stephen was very stressed during this time. He was extremely ill, and it transpired that he had a tumour on his brain. This was successfully removed but has left him deaf in his left ear. At this point, I have to say, that Stephen seemed distant. I often thought that he wasn't interested in anything I had to talk about, until I discovered that he was deaf, but he had been trying to hide it.

He still follows his closeness to the church, but never pushes his beliefs on anyone. Stephen met his second wife at a church picnic. He saw an attractive lady with four young daughters and offered her a ride home in his car. Stephen also offered to help her if she ever needed it. After a long romance Stephen and Linda got married. Stephen sold his small house, and moved into Linda's one, using his money to build an extension, adding a bigger lounge, kitchen, laundry room, shower, and an extra bedroom.

Stephen and Linda have two sons together, Jorden and Christian. Stephen has six children altogether, and four stepdaughters from his second marriage, with too many grandchildren to mention and he loves all of them. He regularly visits Christopher, who now lives in Slovenia with his wife, Marcella, and two children, and takes annual trips to Majorca where Jeremy lives with his wife, Heidi.

During Mum's later years Stephen spent a lot of time with her, taking her shopping, and for walking trips down to the River Severn where it merges with the River Avon, or popping into Mum's favourite café for coffee. Some of Stephen's church friends used to meet for coffee in this café, giving Mum the perfect opportunity to air her views on God, all done with an open mind.

Mum and Stephen spent a lot of time together, using each other as sounding boards. When they discussed Mum's funeral together, Mum told Stephen that it didn't matter where it was held. The only place we deemed suitable for our Mum was the abbey! Mum would have felt honoured. Once, when I was staying with her, she received a telephone call. Stephen took it, then called out to me that the caller was David from the abbey. I relayed this message to Mum, 'David from the Abbey National is on the phone!' David from the abbey arrived and gave Mum communion and had a long chat with her.

Stephen age fourteen

The three of us

Stephen and Barbara in Lower Road, Eastbourne

Stephen and Barbara on Eastbourne beach

Proud brother giving his sister away.

CHAPTER TWELVE

My sister, Barbara Avril

My big sister, Barbara Avril, was also born in Eastbourne on 11th April 1946. Another one of Mum's words of wisdom, was 'women with very blonde hair combined with brown eyes were coveted by the Romans'. Apparently, on conquering Britain, they described them as 'true English beauties. This was Barbara and I! Whereas blonde women with blue eyes were descendants of the Vikings and dark-haired women with dark eyes were descended from the Irish.

We were very different characters. I never remember Barbara being naughty, unlike me! Barbara always kept herself to herself; she had her friends and I had mine. As children we shared a bedroom, often coming to fisticuffs over our individual spaces but we always ended up friends, falling about laughing, as we couldn't even remember what the argument was about.

Barbara and I shared a love of dogs, especially whippets, but not of horses. They were a bit scary for her; she liked them, but horses were not her bag. However,

Barbara became a well-known breeder and exhibitor of whippets. She also had springer spaniels that she trained for the gun and was often called upon to take her dogs to pheasant shoots at Luton Hoo country mansion. Walking several dogs at a time kept Barbara fit and slim.

Barbara is a psychic medium, having studied the art for many years. She is also a clairvoyant. Once Barbara asked me what the weather would be like next February in Phuket. In a moment of sarcasm I replied, "You're the clairvoyant, you can tell me!" Barbara has also had several books, poems and songs published.

After dating several boys, Barbara married Richard Burgess, her school sweetheart, and they have been married now for 55 years. Barbara and Richard have two daughters. Larissa lives in Australia and is a nurse and a midwife. She has made a wonderful life for herself in Australia. Barbara's younger daughter, Selina, is a world class swimmer, swimming for England abroad. Selena was short-listed for the Sidney Olympics, and even got measured for the uniform!

For her career path Selina chose to be a teacher of science. Selina met Ross through their mutual love of swimming. Ross competes in long distance swimming, sometimes for the army, and sometimes as a personal challenge. He has swum around Jersey and he currently holds the world record time for this. Ross and Selina married and now have two children.

Barbara visited me here in Phuket with Mum, and we had a great time together. The morning of their arrival, Mum appeared in a swimsuit, heading for the swimming pool carrying an inflatable ball; she announced, "it's a buoyancy aid". I assured Mum that the pool wasn't deep, and that there was no need for the ball because an inflatable killer whale lived in the pool. Mum descended the steps into the pool, grabbed hold of the handle of the killer whale, promptly tipping backwards, and going under the water with her feet in the air. Every time Mum surfaced, she was calling out for help, I hurried over. I kept telling her to put her feet down. Barbara, who was in the pool, eventually rescued Mum. Oh dear! I thought that would be the end of Mum's swimming, but no way! Mum was in there every day. She was so funny, and after a few days she was walking around in the pool doing breaststroke with her arms, saying 'I have the hang of this swimming lark: it's easy!'

Mum used to say that Barbara, as a child, was 'different'. We were chatting one day, and Barbara kept gazing to my left, looking distracted. Suddenly, she announced, "I can't concentrate on what we're talking about, there's a little girl sitting next to you on the sofa." Once, the family had attended an award ceremony where Selina was being presented with a swimming trophy. Barbara learned back from the table and said to me,

"Grandma is here with Grandad. Do you want to say hello?" "No," was my answer.

Not having a psychic bone in my body makes it difficult for me to understand Barbara. I confess that I am a sceptic. However, Barbara is very dedicated to being a psychic medium, following it all through her life, and is well known for her ability, which gives me the feeling that she had no choice over this. She was given this gift whether she liked it or not.

Over the years I've grown closer to Barbara, often seeking her advice. She has supported me when the going has been tough, offering a different viewpoint to me.

We were a cheeky pair.

Barbara and I, little angels!

Little angels, bridesmaids at Aunty Dorothy's wedding

Barbara with Lorna and my whippets.

Barbara with Granny at Eastbourne.

Sisters

The three of us.

Barbara and Mum holding the killer whale.

CHAPTER THIRTEEN

Me, my lodgers, and Glen

It must be obvious by now that I am who I am, and what life has made me. With all my difficulties, I guess you could say that I'm grateful because they have all been character-building blocks in my life. I have learned through my mistakes and whatever life has thrown at me, I sincerely hope that it has given me empathy towards others.

My door is always open as I have learned that a problem shared is a problem halved. When people come to me with a life conundrum, I can usually relate to it through my extensive life experiences. One day when, struggling financially and with depression I just couldn't manage to get out of bed, but by lunchtime I was kicking myself up the backside. Hitting the telephone, I called AA. explaining to them that, having two empty bedrooms, I wished to offer a home to a battered wife of an alcoholic. They advised me that they had no women victims on their books at that time and suggested that I try St. Joseph's men's refuge. This I did straight away—no time like the present!

The next day a representative came round to interview me and see what was on offer. At that time, I was living on my own in a three-bedroom house: my own bedroom was downstairs and upstairs, were two further bedrooms and a toilet. They invited me to go to the day centre to meet potential candidates. There I was shown into a small room, and in walked Adrian. We sat opposite each other, and he told me about himself and how he had ended up on the streets. We were given a cup of coffee each, and relaxing back in my chair, I spilt half of my coffee all over myself. "Oh shit!" I exclaimed. Adrian burst out laughing. That was the ice breaker. Decision made—I told the organizer that I didn't need to see anyone else.

Adrian told me later that he knew I was a down to earth woman with no airs and graces. He moved in the next day. I told him to just go upstairs and choose a bedroom. I gave him a key to the house, telling him that I was off to work, and would see him tomorrow. Months later Adrian told me how naively trusting, even stupid I was, to leave him in my house. My answer was a simple one—there were three dogs to get past! Other than that, if they could find anything of value in the house, and were that desperate, they were welcome! In my absence *anyone* could have burgled; me, how could they be stopped?

In no time at all a second lodger moved in. Then I had a phone call one evening, asking if I could take in a third young man who was so desperate for a place to stay that he slept on a camp bed in my conservatory.

I always felt safe, and my house had never been so clean and tidy!

CHAPTER FOURTEEN

How Thailand and Kingsacre came about.

I had first visited Nai Yang 35 years earlier, and had met and befriended a Thai lady there called Sumali, who was a widow with a 10-year-old son, Pong. Back in those days Nai Yang, Phuket and Thailand had yet to be discovered as a holiday destination. But I anticipated that the future was going to be tourism and, to help Sumali to secure a good future, I encouraged Pong to learn to speak English. To help him we started to write letters to each other, and we exchanged photos. Through circumstances, I did not return until 10 years later. Pong was still there working in a tourist kiosk on the beach. Sumali had progressed from a makeshift wok kitchen in a sidecar, to a rough wooden shack of which she was immensely proud.

Glen and I had had several holidays in Nai Yang, often staying with a Thai friend instead of a hotel. Once we made the decision to retire to Thailand we asked Pong if he could find us some land on which to build a house.

He had contacts and local knowledge, and while he was searching, Glen and I went on a 'live aboard' dive trip. Now anyone reading this will be thinking, 'whoops, silly people!' Yes, for sure we had heard of foreigners being duped out of money. However, *this was Me*. I trusted Pong.

He found the land for us that is now Kingsacre, suggesting that we gave him the money so that he would buy the land then transfer it into our names Oh no!' said our lawyer. She advised us to start a company. We took her advice, and Kingsacre Company Limited was created. We started this company in order to buy the land in the company name and are now co-directors of Kingsacre. Naturally, we made Pong a shareholder and put him in charge of the construction. We had the land blessed by the local abbot who decreed that we should turn the first *sod* and put in the first building post at 6am on 29th September, 2003.

We returned to the UK and after a month we had a call from Pong saying that the first house was half built and second house started, and could I please send him more money, so I transferred over £5,000. Two weeks later, another request for money came, and another £5,000 was winging its way over to our Thai bank account, which Pong had access to in order to pay the builder and materials.

Then we received an alarming call from Sumali telling us not to send any more money; she would explain it all in a letter. Glen was on the next flight over, only to find a shell of a half-built house, but nothing else and an empty bank account. Pong had robbed us of all our cash. With the help of our lawyer, we pursued Pong to get him arrested. We soon realised that his mother was the one who was being chased to sell her modest house in order to pay us back the 1.2 million baht (£25,000) owed us. We just couldn't do that to her with a clear conscience. This resulted in us throwing good money after bad. We had to move on but we were devastated. To enable us to continue with our 'dream' we had no option but to take out a loan on the apartment. The house here was built in a modest style; we didn't need a showy house. or a glass mansion. Before we moved here to Thailand, Glen and I were working to raise the money lost. I worked night duties, Glen worked a seven day week, so we became 'ships passing in the night'.

We moved to Nai Yang, and I suddenly found Glen and I, 24/7 in each other's space. Predictably we both had valid ideas for the building and running of Kingsacre, but that situation created a certain amount of friction between us. And that's putting it lightly! All the same, we managed to build a very successful holiday resort that attracted returning guests year after year, and we eventually expanded, even buying some neighbouring land to offer camping facilities, bamboo cabins and then a self-contained cottage named Palm Cottage in memory of a dear friend, Robert Palmer, who had unfortunately taken his own life, leaving me bereft of his company and sunny smile.

Glen was leading a double life for a long time, claiming to be impotent to me while seeking 'it' elsewhere, or should I say anywhere! He had found his paradise with all it had to offer! All this was brought to my attention by a woman who had been having an affair with Glen for three years in full knowledge of my existence! Many women have been to see Kingsacre, and fantasize about becoming 'its mistress'. It later became known that this woman had spent time together with Glen at Kingsacre whilst I was away doing flight volunteer work to Toronto and New York for Soi Dog, a charity for the welfare of stray dogs and cats in Asia. No wonder Glen encouraged me to do this. He tried very hard to get me to go away on a dive trip at Christmas. Once he had dumped this particular lady, it led her to send me a graphic account of what had gone on, including visits to sex clubs, swinging, threesomes, and prostitutes.

They say beware a woman scorned. Hell, hath no fury! Never mind me! This woman had definitely been scorned. She couldn't wait to tell me all about it once he had dumped her. But I was made of stronger stuff; this did not break me! I was disgusted, hurt, shocked, bewildered, but not broken hearted. After all, following on from my previous marriage failure, I had vowed that no-one could or would ever do that to me again. As a result of all this I have a very thick skin. It's a shame that the soft, loving person inside me is now hidden, a 'fortress of my heart' as Sting put it. Sorry to say that, due to a lifetime of depression my glass has always been half empty; I don't seem able to focus on what is good about my life, and allow the bad times to dominate me.

CHAPTER FIFTEEN

Dogs, my salvation

As mentioned, the first time I came to Phuket was more than three decades ago. There were fewer tourists back then and it was still considered a relatively new destination. There were lots of packs of what seemed to be wild dogs. On my return the following year, there were hardly any dogs, and in my naive ignorance I assumed that they had been disposed of. How, was my next question. A few years later when I returned again, I discovered to my horror that there was a government dog pound.

I heard graphic descriptions of the conditions in which the dogs were kept after being rounded up and impounded there. The word was that tourists *'didn't like them'* and were afraid of attacks! In direct comparison, it did not take long for me to discover about a couple who were driving around in a pick-up truck feeding and treating sick and hungry so-called 'wild' dogs. That intrigued me. Finding out more about this, was my mission, so I looked into it. John and Gill Dalley, an

English couple, who, like us had come to Phuket to retire, had their lives turned upside down by the plight of these dogs.

Through massive fundraising they managed to secure a piece of land to operate from which they created the now Worldwide Soi Dog Foundation at Mai Kao, close to the island's international airport. Soi means 'Street,' so Soi dogs is "Street Dogs". Their mission was to 'catch, neuter and return' stray dogs to where they were found, thus reducing the ever-exploding dog population. The Soi Dog Foundation has grown beyond anyone's wildest dreams, from the back of a pick-up truck to the phenomenal worldwide-renowned charitable dog rescue organization it is today! They now even have a purpose-built school room, where school children attend extracurricular classes dedicated to educating new generations into a better understanding of animals, and the cruelty through ignorance that they have suffered in the past. There the children are allowed to interact with the puppies under supervision.

Gill Dalley was voted Asian 'Woman of the Year' for two years running. It had never been previously known for this award to go to a non-Asian candidate. Gill passed away some years back. Nevertheless her legacy still lives on. Soi Dogs is now, the *"Gill Dalley Soi dog Foundation"*.

After moving to the island, I decided that being without a dog was not for me, and it was only natural for me to go to the Soi Dog Centre with a mind to adopt a dog. I looked at three canine candidates but decided that they were not quite what I was looking for. Just as I was at the point of leaving, a scruffy, sad-looking white dog caught my eye. I asked if I could take a look, but the staff member said that she was sick. She was in the hospital run with three other poorly dogs. Nevertheless, she was calling to me. The keeper got her out for me. We looked into each other's eyes, she licked my hand and she melted my heart. The deal was done there and then. She had to come home with me. I wanted her and she needed me. The keeper kept repeating that she was sick. "That's not a problem for me," I told her. "I'll take over her care and treatment, and that will create a space for another needy dog."

Her name was Tamarind. Her story was that she had been found in a terrible state on the streets of Phuket Town. After I got her home, it took three days for her to come out of her box without me pulling the mat that she was laying on, just to take her for a wee. She didn't eat or drink. Glen was away on a trip to the UK, so Tam and I were alone, and it was quiet. I decided to move her into the house with me, as it wasn't having the desired effect with her sleeping out on the patio (I had thought she would feel more comfortable outdoors, being a street dog). But after I had gently walked her round the garden, and led her into the house, she immediately went and sat in a corner. I put a cushion there for her. It was another five days before one evening she walked over to sit by me for a few minutes before returning to her cushion. This was extended to the point where she would stay under my feet which were on a footstool. From that moment on this was Tam's permanent place of residence—under my feet.

It took three full years of treatment for her mange and fungal infections to clear up. The only effective drug that kills mange mites was given by injection weekly. It would clear up, only to return again three months later. The poor little thing was ill more than she was well. Someone suggested that I should administer the drug in her food but she wouldn't eat when she was ill, so that advice, although, well meant, didn't work. One time she was banging her head during the night because the mange mites in her head were driving her insane. She looked awful and was bleeding, with eyes swollen shut. It was dreadful to sit with her. I thought she was dying, and I prayed that it would be quick. But some very sound advice was given to me. I took her to Dr Anucha, a vet in Chalong on the east coast of the island, who specialized in skin problems. The drug was given in a syringe mixed with milk daily. That was the turning point in Tam's recovery. She never looked back, and the mange never returned. Tam grew into the most incredible canine companion I have ever known.

During this time, I wanted to help the dogs at the dog pound. Frankly, I was scared of what I might see. I had heard that the conditions were horrendous, dogs dying daily through gangs/packs of dogs homing in on a victim or sick young dogs. With over 1,500 dogs incarcerated at the pound this worried me. I contacted a lady called Toni Jessup, who helped there. I told her of my fears and she arranged to meet me there to show me around. The place had already been improved by John and Gill's foundation. The runs now had concrete floors instead of mud, making it easier to keep clean and large covered shelters had been built. There were also large drainpipes where dogs could hide from trouble. It was still far from perfect and yes, dogs did die, but not at anywhere near the previous rates.

I was soon volunteering, going on a three-times-a-week basis. I was given responsibility, taking charge of what was known as the 'puppy run,' which was attached to other small runs with dogs designated as 'troublemakers' who needed to be separated from the main runs. After cleaning and socialising the puppies, the other dogs got a walk around the car park.

Alexi, a Canadian friend, worked with me for a month while she stayed at Kingsacre. Alexi and I are firm friends. The need for help went out and several people joined the workforce, some with a long-term commitment, others who were simply passing through; I salute you all. Leoni,

Quami, and Mark were there working what hours they could. They were soon joined by Holly and Gina, Colin, Barbara and Malisa, Toni and Allen. Oh gosh! There are too many to name them all. From my perspective, I could see the problems where 'rich' foreigners would swan in to help, which in itself was a slap in the face to the Thai workers who did what they could for the minimum pay. Politics was a problem up at the shelter to the point that volunteers were discouraged. Due to bouts of distemper followed by COVID-19, only a select few regular workers were allowed in. I was not one of them!

At Kingsacre, a lady called Jessica Kelly stayed with us. The first time we met she had flown over from Toronto to be a 'flight volunteer' for the foundation. This made me very interested in looking into flight volunteer work. Becoming inspired, I was prompted to go on my first flight volunteer trip, I flew with six dogs to Toronto where they had been adopted. Four of the dogs originated from the dog pound and had been selected by Toni and taken into foster care to prepare them for a new life. In Bangkok. I was joined by two more dogs waiting to go from another rescue group. The flight took us across to Taiwan, then across the Pacific Ocean and on to the USA. Now I can truly say that I have been around the world.

There was no way that I could possibly go to Toronto without meeting up with Jessica. She drove down to the airport in the middle of the night to collect me. I stayed with her and her partner, Brent, for a week. They are the most amazing people who train and breed Dutch Malinois dogs, setting a very high standard, for police work, army service, sniffer dogs and more. That is their domain. Heading up all this, Jessica has her own gorgeous service dog called Kitty. They never ceased to amaze me! Thirteen dogs in the house, all remarkably well trained. They are very inspiring people.

Later I took three dogs to New York for private adoption. On this occasion, I flew from Bangkok to Moscow then across the Atlantic Ocean to New York. Being nosy and not paying attention, I stupidly fell off the airplane as I was disembarking. I was very embarrassed having to go the rest of the way in a wheelchair. Sightseeing in New York on my own, in the cold with a painful ankle was not my idea of fun. I even paid to go into a museum just to sit down and get warm. Yes, I managed to get around, but it was pretty much all on the subway, so as you can imagine, I didn't see much, but I did manage to take a few selfies standing in strategic places doing the touristy thing. Rachel, the lady who had organised this particular trip paid for me to see a Broadway show. I chose "Beautiful," the story of Carol King. it was in a small theatre up a side street, very intimate and full to the hilt. .

Following the death of my dearest dog, Tam, at the age of thirteen I started to go to Soi Dog to fill the hole in my life. Previously, when I had adopted Tam, I had been doing voluntary work remotely. This fitted in well with me running Kingsacre as it included taking in foreign volunteers at a reduced price. Now I had been assigned to the small dog run, to walk the dogs. I made some new friends at Soi Dogs, namely, Owen, Sylvie, and Yanisa. Here I would like to add that whenever changes within an organization occur it doesn't always go down well; people don't like change! I have witnessed many changes at Soi Dogs, without having been a part of them, rather looking in from outside. I've seen Soi Dogs grow tremendously. I would like to say a thank you to Louise Rose, the new CEO, for doing a difficult job in the best possible way.

I had no intention of getting another dog, but it wasn't long before a sweet little boy called George caught my eye. Most of the small dogs nearly pulled me off my feet (even three legged ones) just to get to the off-lead area where they could run free and play for a while, often not wanting to go back in again. George, however, walked at my side. He was a very gentle little dog. When it was time to go back to the run, he came to call, sat down, raised his front paw and licked my hand. I am convinced that Tam must have whispered a word or two in his ear. I was instantly smitten.

The dogs had to be walked in their pecking order, top dog first. George was number six in line to walk. I couldn't wait, and soon I was expressing a desire to adopt him. I set the ball rolling for his adoption, and tomorrow will be his first-year anniversary of living with me. While I waited for the documents to get done, I researched his history. I was told that he was 5 years old and had been transferred over to Soi Dogs from the dog pound after being very badly attacked by other dogs. One of the victims of the pack, Mark Shaw, recognized his photo on my Facebook page and asked, 'Is that George?' He remembered him being dumped there as a puppy. Gina and Holly told me how he was constantly being attacked. He had actually learned how to climb up the mesh fencing away from gnashing teeth, but this resulted in his back legs being bitten and torn. George spent 4 years at the pound, then 6 months at Soi being treated for dog bites, until he caught my attention.

I have found him to be a very sweet natured little dog, very quiet and affectionate. Unfortunately, George suffers from separation anxiety and he howls his head off, and has ripped our gate to shreds several times, whenever I pop out. Thanks to Curtis (the Soi dogs, dog behaviourist) I now have a strategy to overcome this. If he does get out when I have been shopping he is very pleased to greet me on my return. I am sure that he is saying, "Aren't I a clever boy to get out to meet you?" I have discovered that he has a very big fear of the night-time, and have observed him getting anxious as the evenings close in, especially when it is raining, and he is traumatized by thunder. I can only surmise that bad things must have happened to him under the cover of darkness; maybe dog gangs getting into howling frenzies due to the rain and thunder and the atmospheric pressure, and probably more. I am convinced that George can detect changes in the atmosphere prior to a storm. Never mind, he has a cubby hole to call his own now.

George has been joined by Lilly, a street dog that wandered into our lives. She was very thin and frightened, but now she and George are so in love. George has a soul mate and has learned how to play-fight with her without fear. Occasionally Lilly gets too keen, but the slightest squeak from George and she lets go and starts to lick him, hence her name is 'Likin' Lilly. 'Both dogs are prepped to go to England with me.

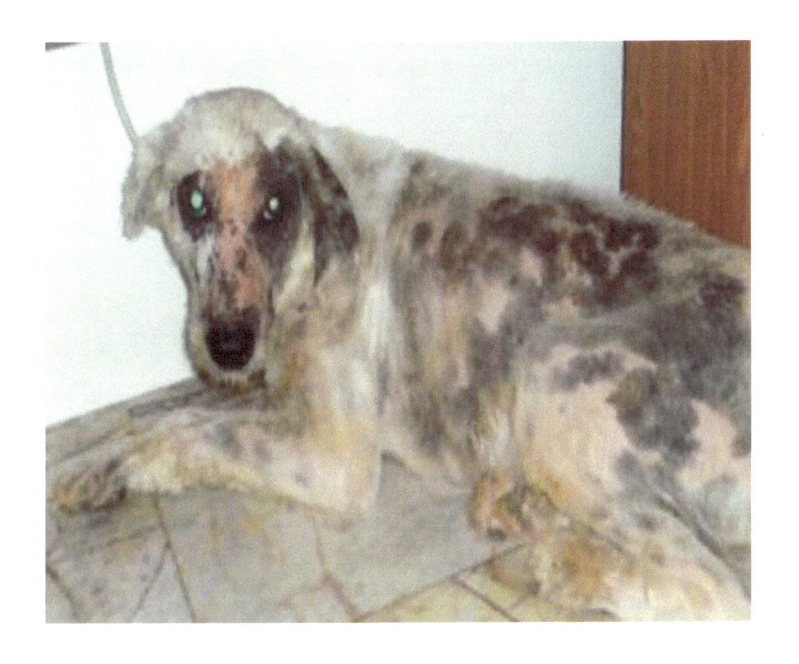

Tam on arrival, sick and afraid.

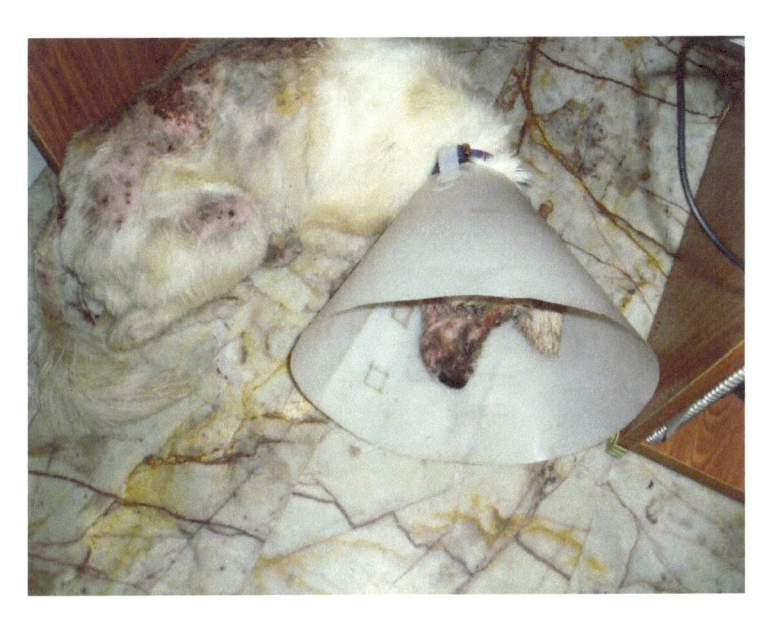

Three years later, my loving and faithful companion.

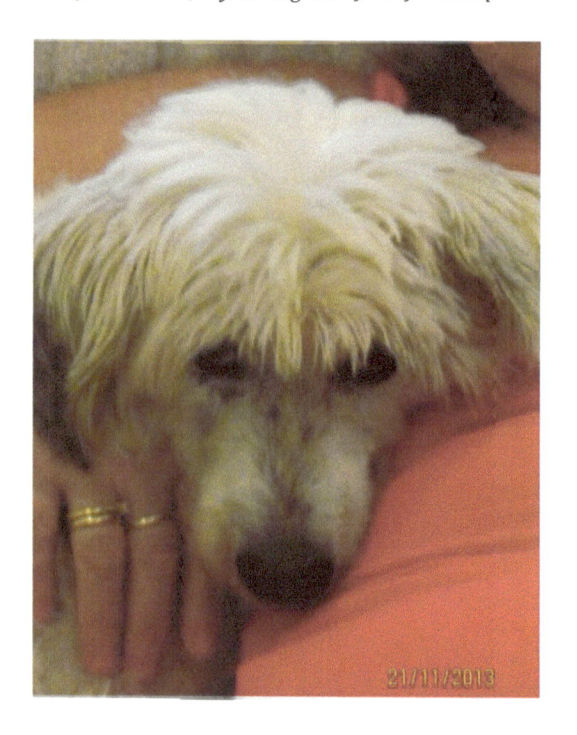

Who is that beautiful dog looking up at me?

Loading the dogs to fly to Toronto.

*Kennel Maid! Cleaning the dog run.
My teacher said this is what I wanted to be when I was 9.*

Arrival day for the start of a new life.

Are you coming to bed, mum

George and his soul mate, his play fighting friend.

Lickin' Lilly on Nai Yang beach
Her first time out on a lead

EPILOGUE

MOVING ON, A NEW LIFE. RETURNING TO MY ROOTS.

The lengthy process of moving from Phuket in Thailand started in November 2022. I had already adopted George and subsequently adopted Lillie who had appeared on the neighbouring land from the jungle. She was young looking, very thin and frightened. I suspected that she had not been sterilized, so contacted Soi Dogs to come and collect her for that process. To help in her capture I started to leave food out for her, and slowly she became less fearful. Lillie and George quickly became friends and soul mates, and the decision to adopt Lillie was a forgone one. Therefor the decision to take them both with me to England was a simple one.

George was already some way through the lengthy process, so I knew what had to be done. First, Lillie had to be fully inoculated including for rabies. She also had to be microchipped and start the process of having a Titler test done. This is a blood test that must be sent to the laboratories in Europe for confirmation that she has been inoculated against rabies and free from the disease. The first step was to have her fully inoculated, with a booster to follow, then the blood is separated into serum and sent to Brussels. It takes up to three months to complete this, and the certificate is then sent back and lasts her lifetime, providing she continues to have annual boosters. George already has the certificate.

The next step is to plan the journey. Dogs cannot fly directly into the United Kingdom from abroad; they must travel through a European country first. I soon discovered that I wasn't able to book a flight and the follow-on journey without help.

It's not what you know but who you know!

Having done voluntary work with Phuket's many stray dogs I met a few knowledgeable people, who regularly send dogs around the world and to the UK. One such person was Patric. I first met him some years ago when he helped one of my friends to send a rescue dog from Thailand to the UK, and then on to Australia. Patric was amazing in doing this huge task. I also found it difficult to find an airline that I could fly with to Amsterdam. I was expected to buy the ticket and then add the dogs as excess luggage. I was feeling uncomfortable about doing this, so Patric recommended a friend of his who would do it for me. Phew! It took a few weeks to find the right flight, which was Phuket to Istanbul, then on to Amsterdam, a 20-hour journey. Add on to this, a 3-hour period to be checked in, during which time the dogs had to be taken out of their crates, to enable the empty crates to be x-rayed, and also please bear in mind that George and Lillie had spent the previous two years living with only me in a quiet huge garden! They had never been near the airport nor seen so many people gathered and the noise for them was almost unbearable; their crates were the only place where they felt safe.

I lined their crates with incontinence pads in case of accidents, and I had added an old dirty T-shirt and a piece of their old bedding. Patric secured a drinking water bottle to the door. I had spent many weeks trying to teach George and Lillie to accept meat that was wrapped around the nozzle. I even put chicken stock in the bottles to tempt them but I never achieved the point of the exercise where they drank the water from it.

Patric was amazing. Not only had he collated all the paperwork, he picked me and the dogs up, took us to the airport and never left our side. He even checked us all in. This documentation included an export licence, to obtain which it was necessary to take the dogs up to the airport livestock department, for their documents to be checked and be photographed and their micro-chips to be verified. Patric arranged for the Licencing Officer to come to our home to carry this procedure out. Once George and Lillie were taken away to be loaded onto the aircraft, I had a big hug from Patric, and he wished us well in our new life.

I boarded the airplane with nervous anxiety for the dogs, but with no other option we all three had to get through it together. In Istanbul there was a 3 hour layover. Then boarding an airplane to Amsterdam was the next leg of this momentous journey. The approach to Amsterdam was met with the highest of head winds. I have flown around the world many times but have never experienced turbulence like this. The plane dipped up and down, side to side, climbing and falling, and when the captain finally landed the plane all of the passengers applauded.

We were met at Amsterdam airport by Helena, a lady who had stayed with me in Thailand for three months and had met George and Lillie, and she had offered meet us. When the dog crates were unloaded, it was obvious that George had been extremely distressed because his bedding was shredded and ripped up and his water tray had been chewed.

Another friend from Phuket was Melissa. She has a house on Phuket where she stays for months at a time helping at the dog pound and feeding wild street dogs. Melissa offered us a night's stay-over at her other house in Amsterdam, enroute, which was the most amazing and gracious gesture. Not only did Melissa put us up for the night in Amsterdam, and fed us, but she also has a delightful Soi Dog who befriended George and Lillie. I know from what I have learned that dogs live in the moment; the journey was behind them, and they were re-united with me and settled immediately to the situation that they were in. A rescue dog does not live its life saying to itself 'I am a poor rescue dog." Melissa then took us the next morning to her Essex home via the Hook-of-Holland to Harwich, UK, on the ferry.

The ferry was also amazing because they have special cabins for dogs to stay with their owners, and an exercise area. A 7-hour crossing took us to the UK, where we disembarked and drove to Melissa's house for another night's stay. The following morning, we were collected by Gary and driven three more hours to our new abode in Fontwell, Chichester.

CHRISTINE SUSAN MAY

Now seeking a permanent home for us.

On the boat from Amsterdam to England

On the boat deck

In England at last

Snug in our new beds

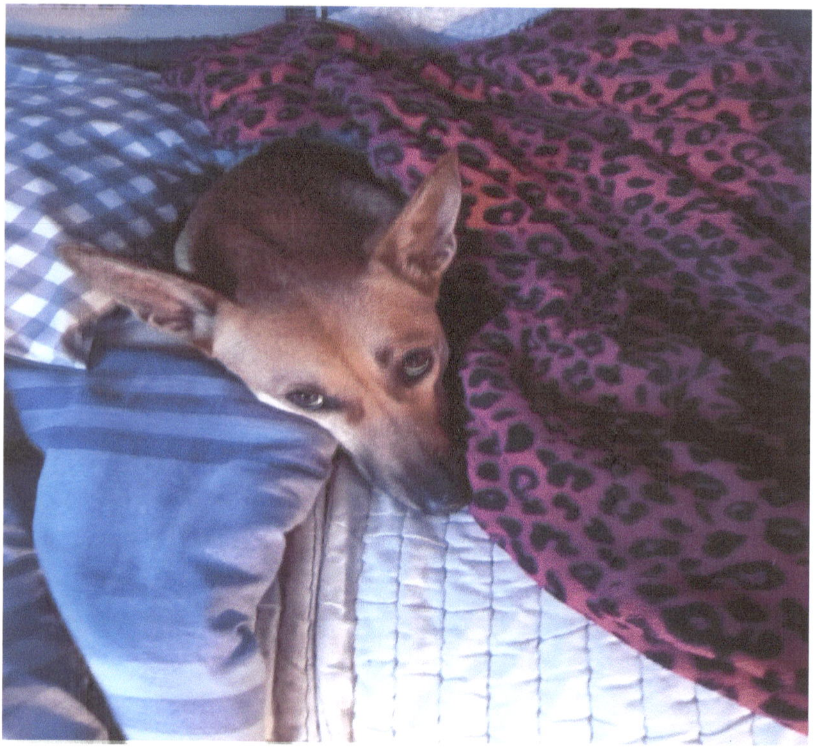

ABOUT THE AUTHOR

The granddaughter of a blacksmith, Christine was born with *horses in her blood.*

Horses, dogs and helping animals has been her lifeblood and helped her through many trials and tribulations.

Written by my sister, Barbara

Milton Keynes UK
Ingram Content Group UK Ltd.
UKHW052141051124
450746UK00001B/15